D1325570

The Playwright

"There are seven subjects
best avoided on television."
  - Dennis Benge

The Playwright

Daren White - story
Eddie Campbell - art

Top Shelf Productions
Knockabout Comics

LEICESTER CITY
LIBRARIES

PAGE 45	05/02/11
	£9.99

The Playwright © &™ 2010 Daren White & Eddie Campbell.
Co-Published by Top Shelf Productions, PO Box 1282 Marietta,
GA 30061-1282 USA. & Knockabout Comics, PO Box 53362,
London NW10 9YX, UK. Top Shelf Productions® and the Top Shelf
logo are registered trademarks of Top Shelf Productions Inc.
All Rights Reserved. This is a work of fiction. Names, characters,
places and incidents are the products of the author's
imagination. Any resemblance to actual events, locales or
persons, living or dead, is entirely coincidental. No part
of this publication may be reproduced without permission
except for small excerpts for purposes of review.
First Printing June 2010. Printed in Singapore.

www.topshelfcomix.com
www.knockabout.com.

The Scenes

Scene One
On the bus

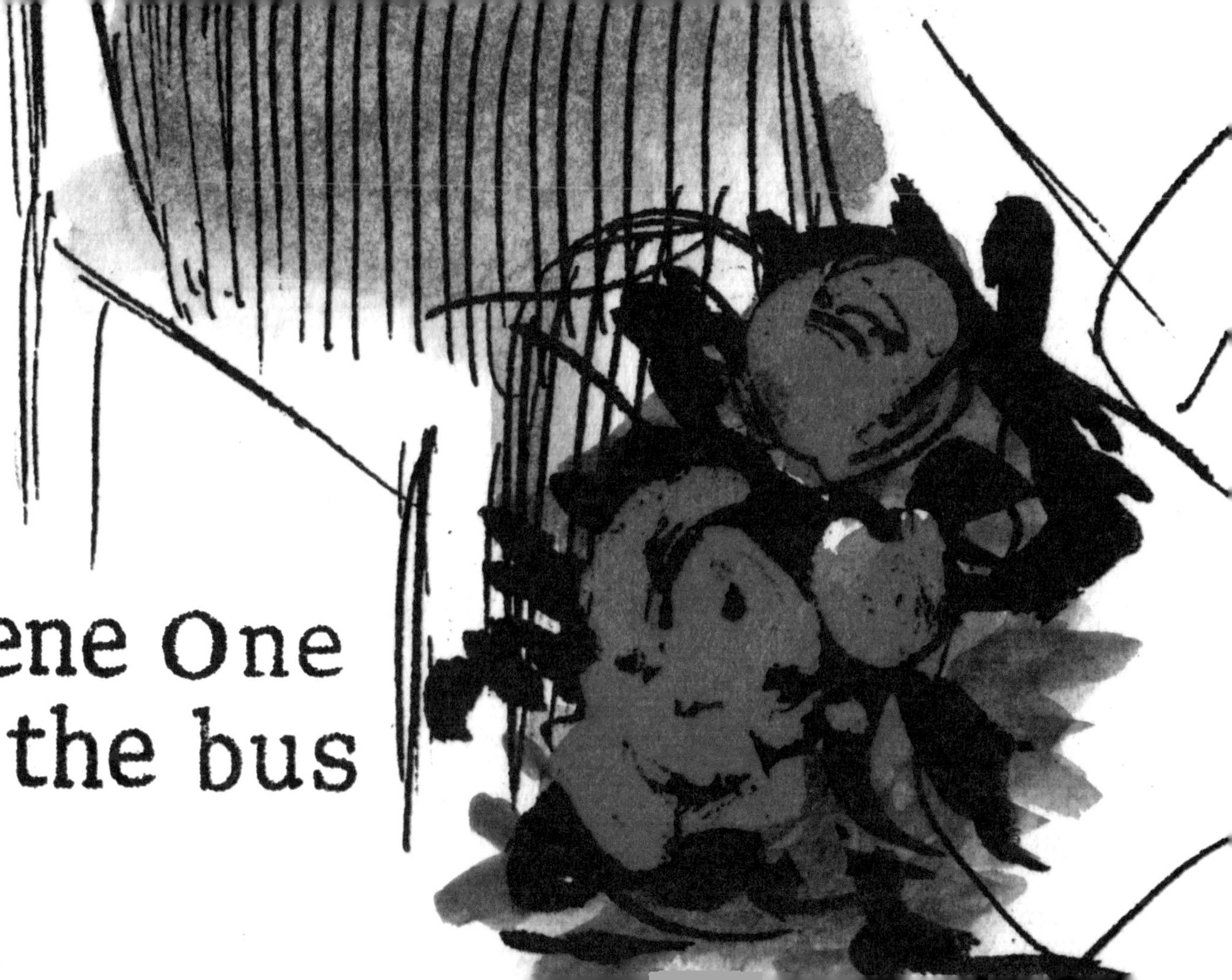

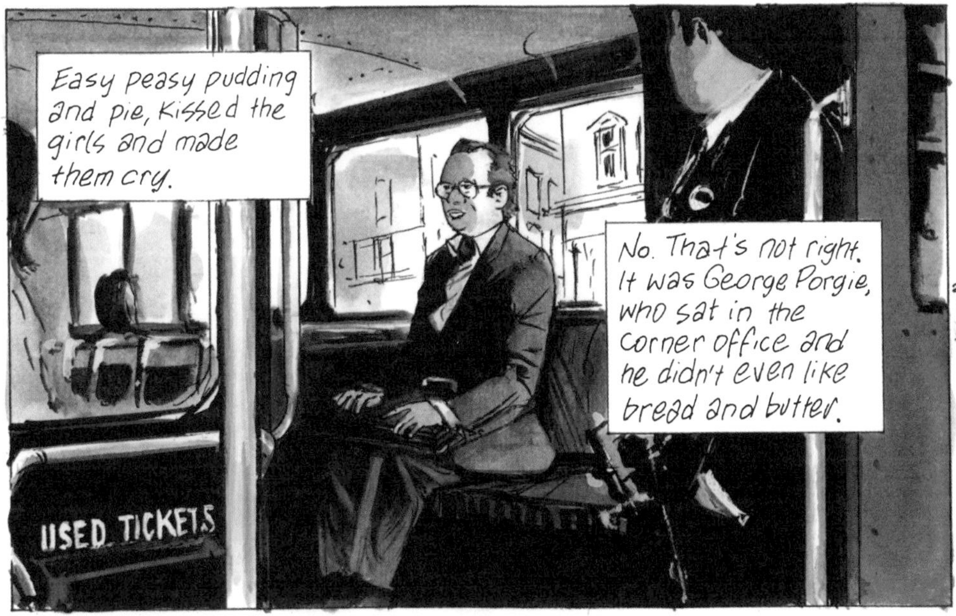
Easy peasy pudding and pie, kissed the girls and made them cry.
No. That's not right. It was George Porgie, who sat in the corner office and he didn't even like bread and butter.
USED TICKETS

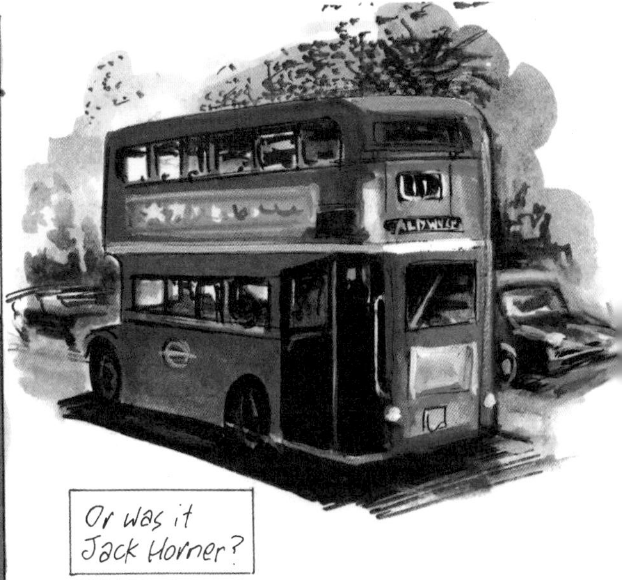
Or was it Jack Horner?

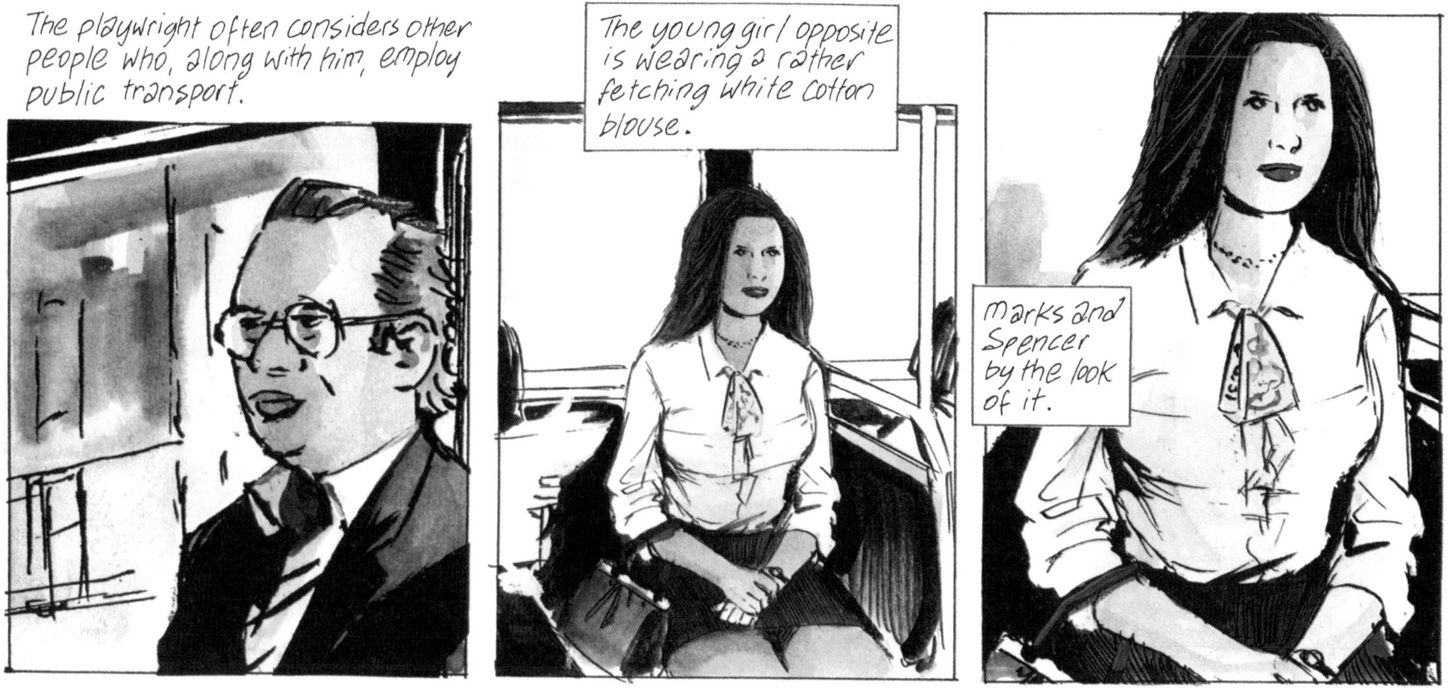
The playwright often considers other people who, along with him, employ public transport.
The young girl opposite is wearing a rather fetching white cotton blouse.
Marks and Spencer by the look of it.

She probably bought it when she got her first job.

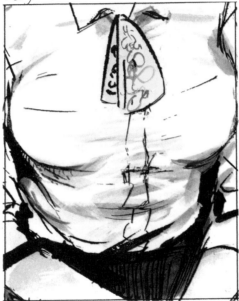

The thing is, she's put on a bit of weight since then.

You can see where the buttons are starting to pull across the chest.

9

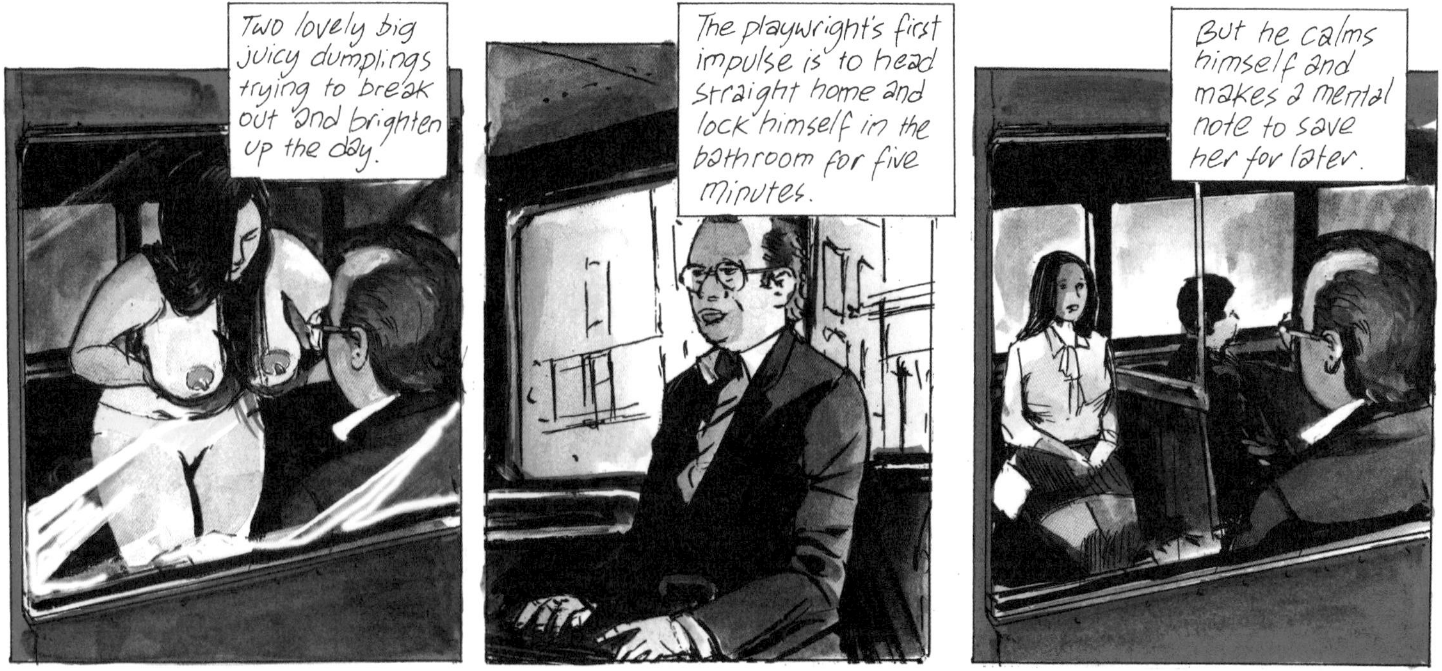
Two lovely big juicy dumplings trying to break out and brighten up the day.
The playwright's first impulse is to head straight home and lock himself in the bathroom for five minutes.
But he calms himself and makes a mental note to save her for later.

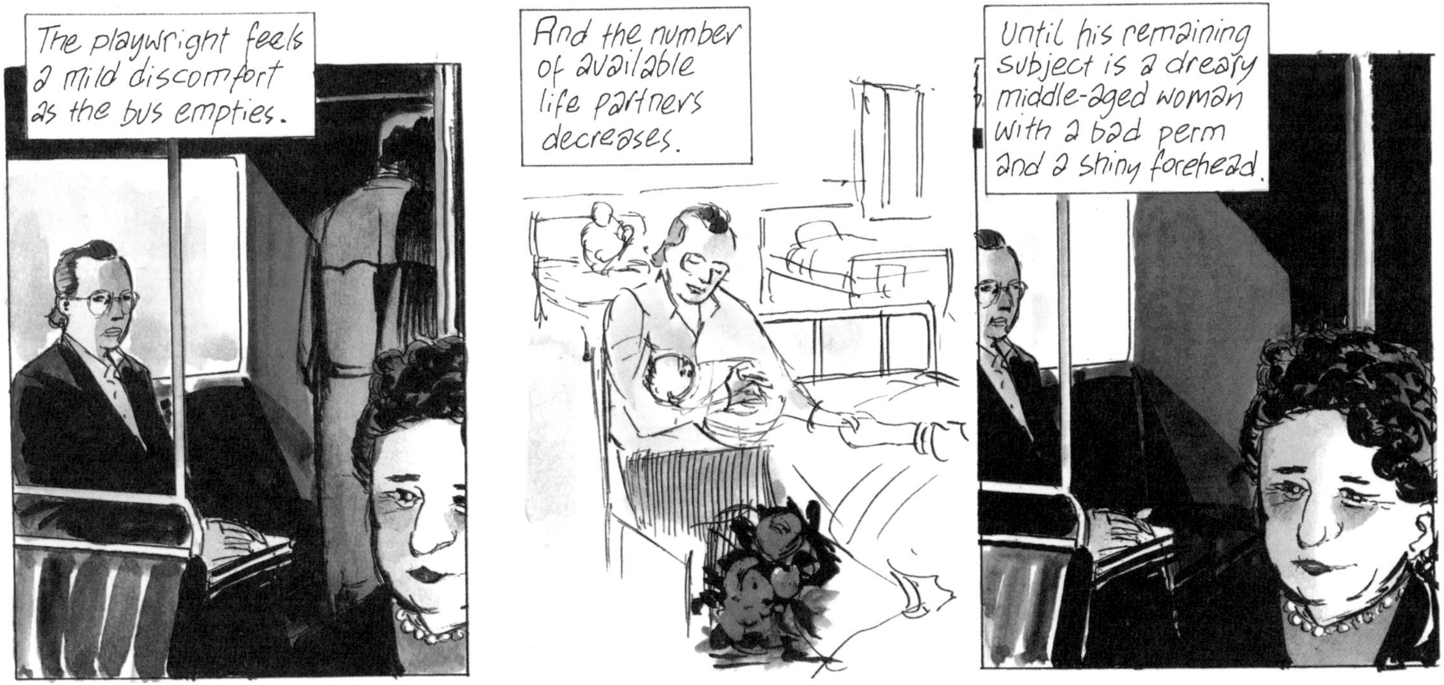
The playwright feels a mild discomfort as the bus empties.
And the number of available life partners decreases.
Until his remaining subject is a dreary middle-aged woman with a bad perm and a shiny forehead.

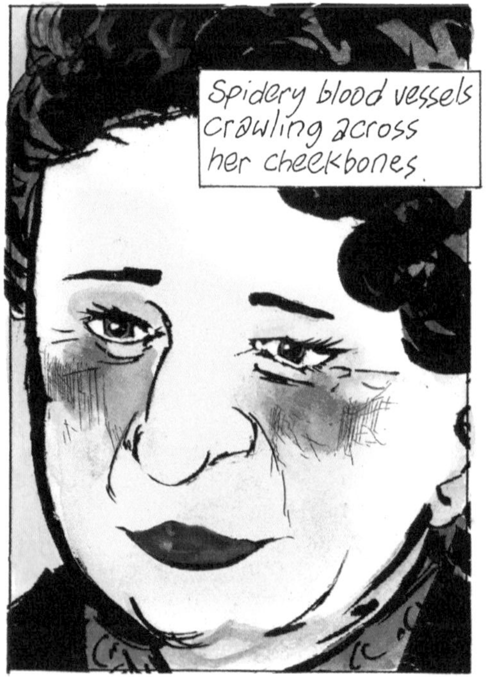
Spidery blood vessels crawling across her cheekbones.

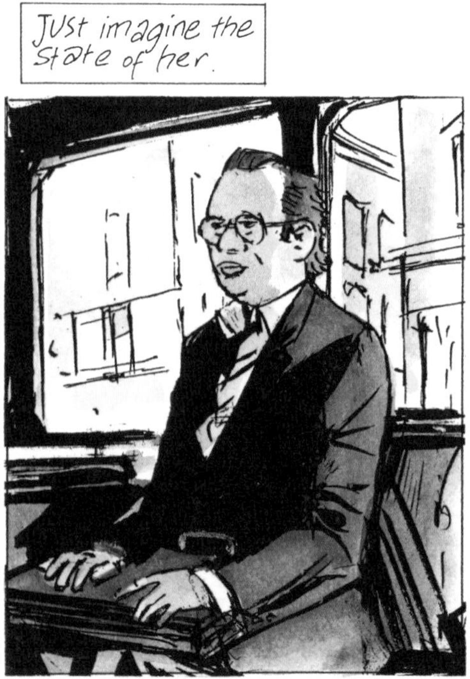
Just imagine the state of her.

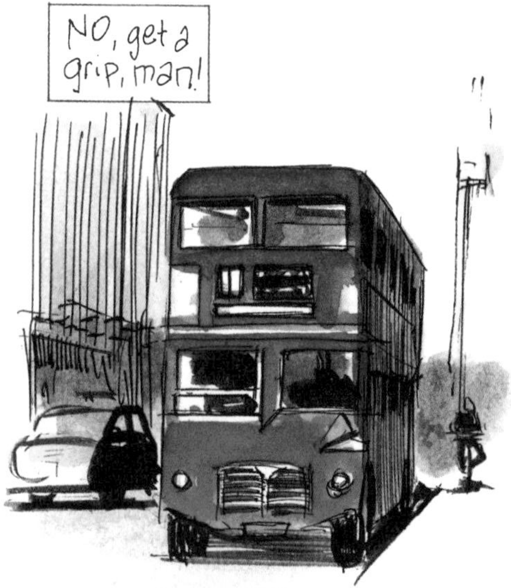
NO, get a grip, man!

The playwright once dated a much younger girl

With whom he struck up a friendship in the local stationers:

He loved the way her hair smelled of marzipan.

and found her ever-so-slightly crossed eyes strangely attractive.

In the parlor of her grandmother's council house, he thought his chance had come.

But he choked and fumbled and fled with embarrassment, never speaking to her again.

He passed the girl in the street, years later.

He thought he might have caught her eye.

But he couldn't be sure.

15

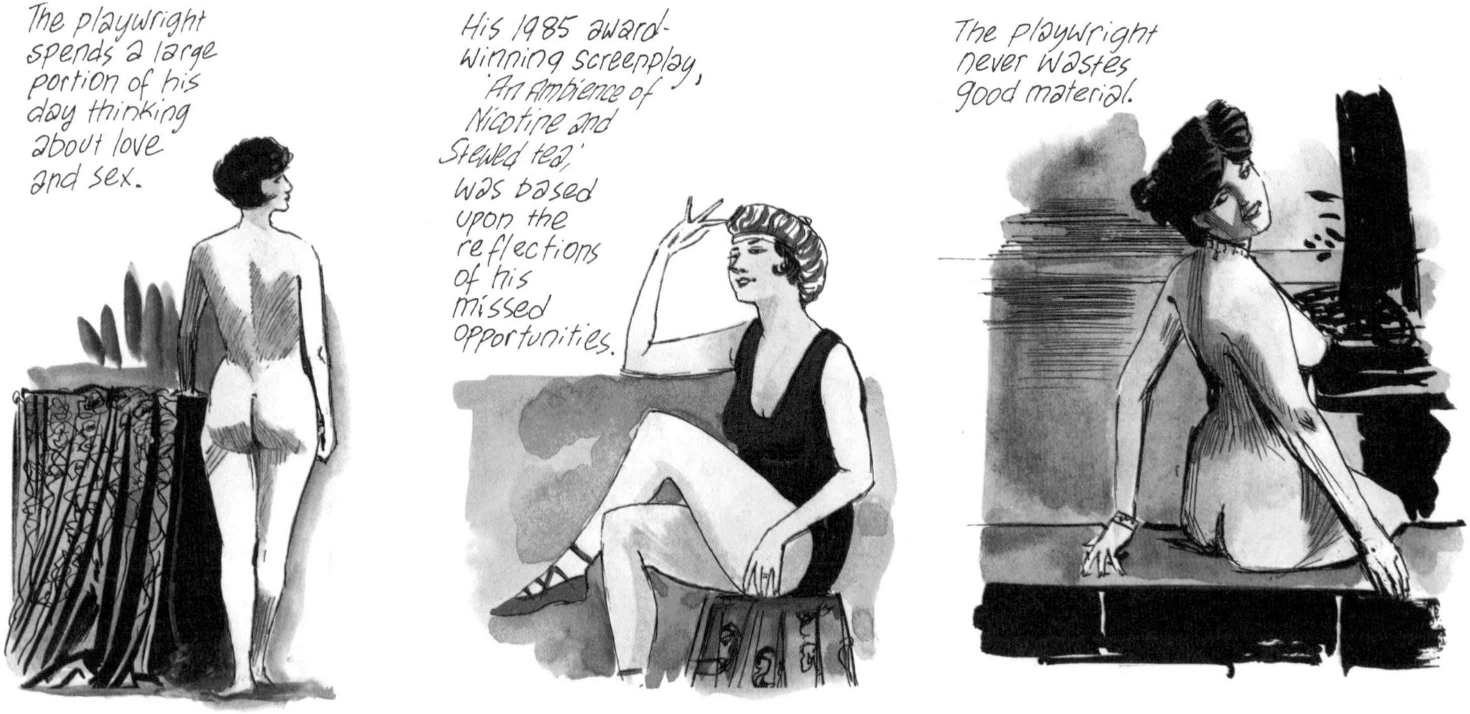
The playwright spends a large portion of his day thinking about love and sex.
His 1985 award-winning screenplay, 'An Ambience of Nicotine and Stewed tea,' was based upon the reflections of his missed opportunities.
The playwright never wastes good material.

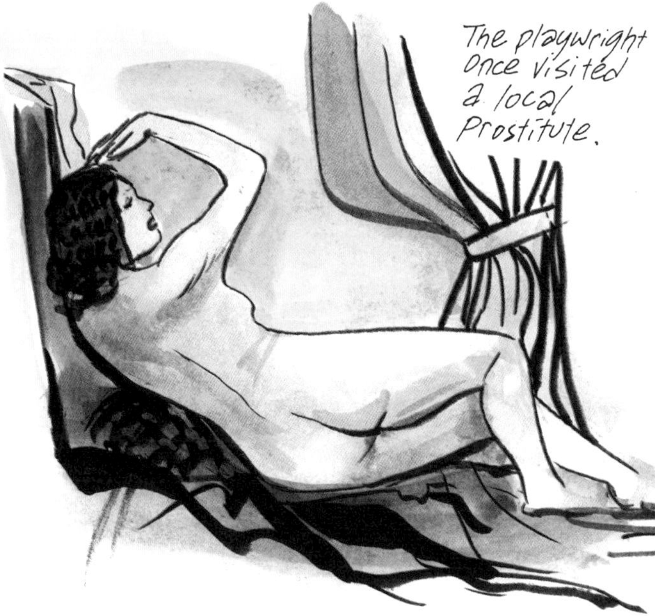
The playwright once visited a local prostitute.

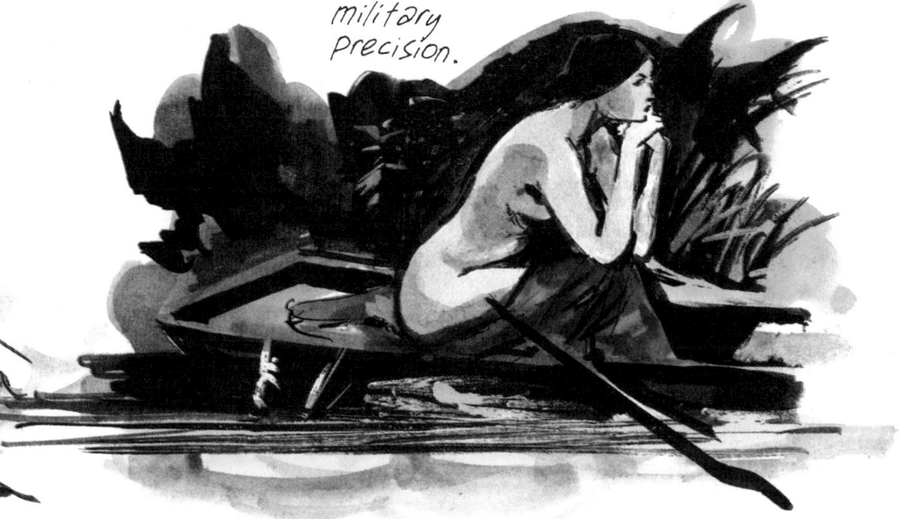
He planned the exercise with military precision.

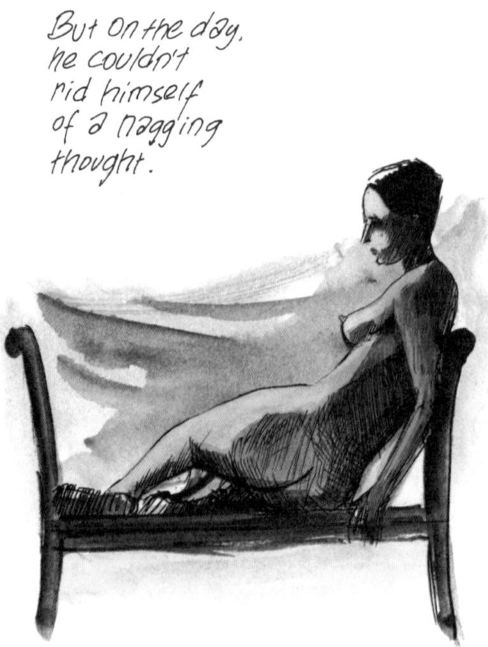
But on the day, he couldn't rid himself of a nagging thought.

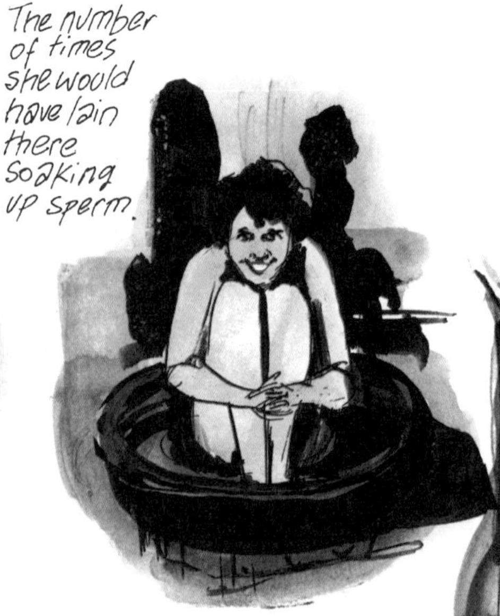
The number of times she would have lain there soaking up sperm.

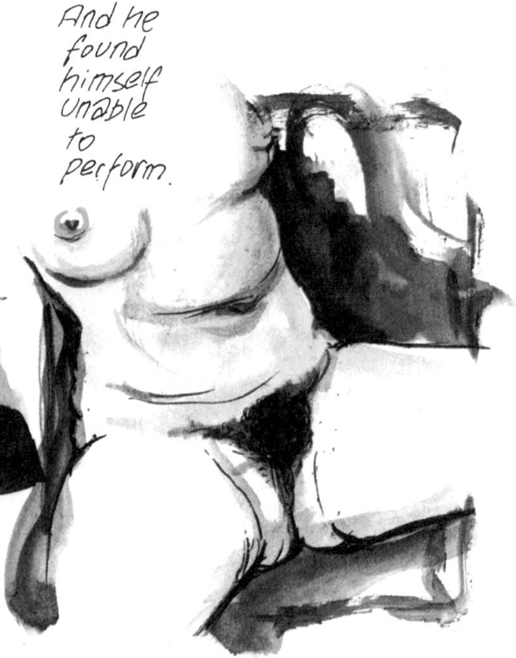
And he found himself unable to perform.

The playwright lodges in Uncle Ernie's spare room.

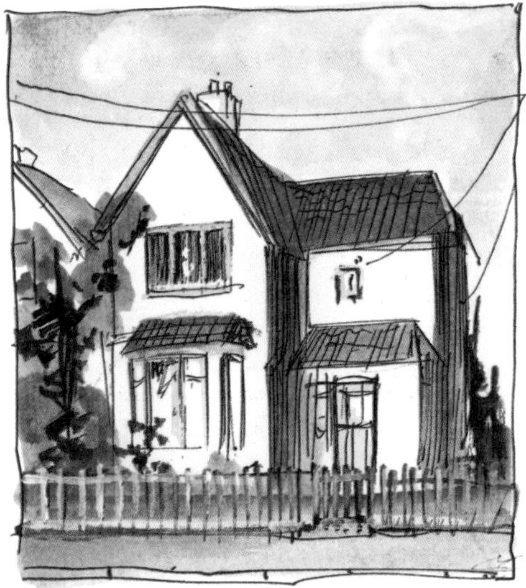

Ernie's real family have long since passed away.

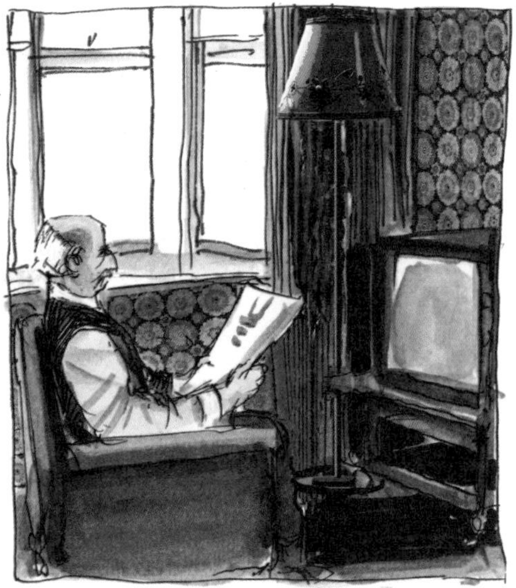

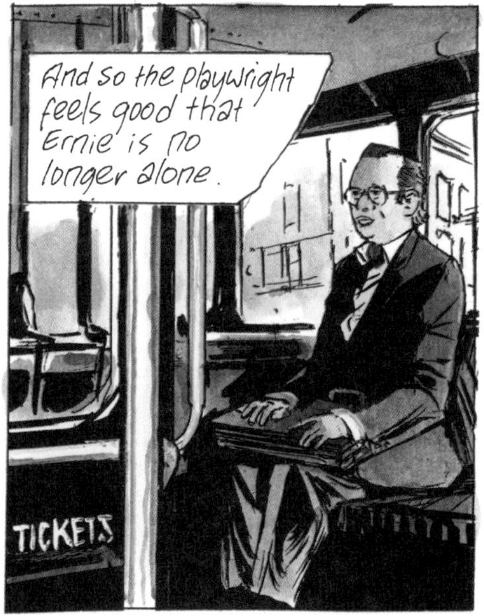
And so the playwright feels good that Ernie is no longer alone.
TICKETS

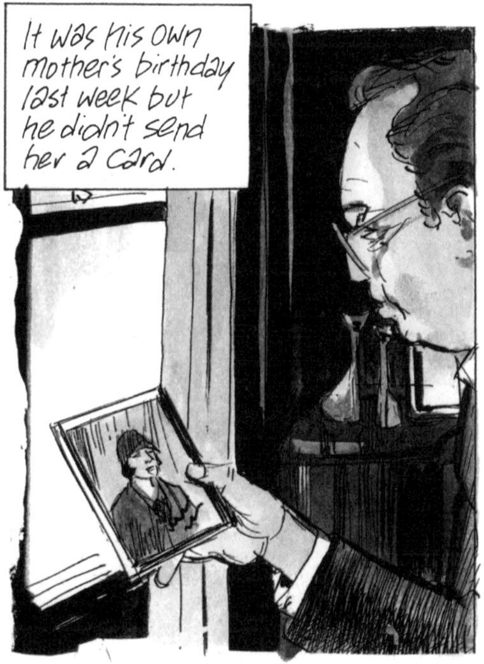
It was his own mother's birthday last week but he didn't send her a card.

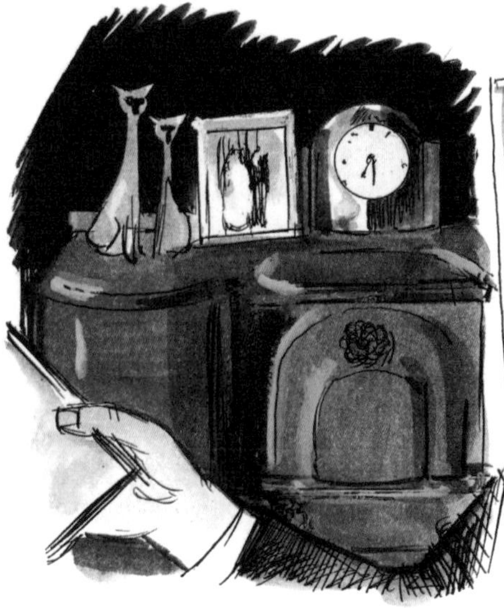
His 1978 award-winning screenplay, 'The Secret' was largely based upon his older, retarded brother.

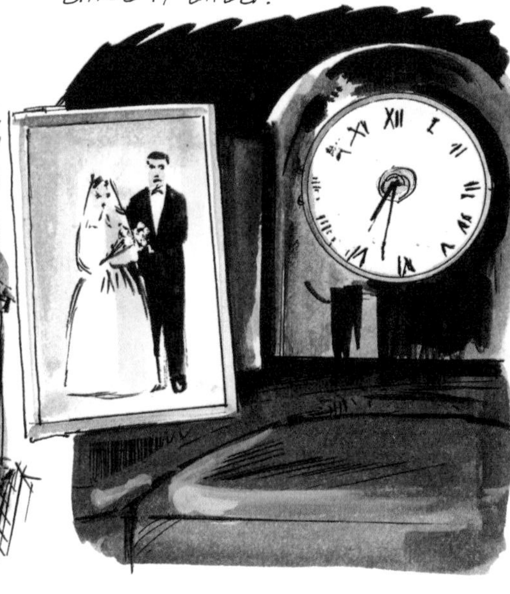
And the playwright hasn't been welcome since it aired.

The playwright regrets
this loss of family.

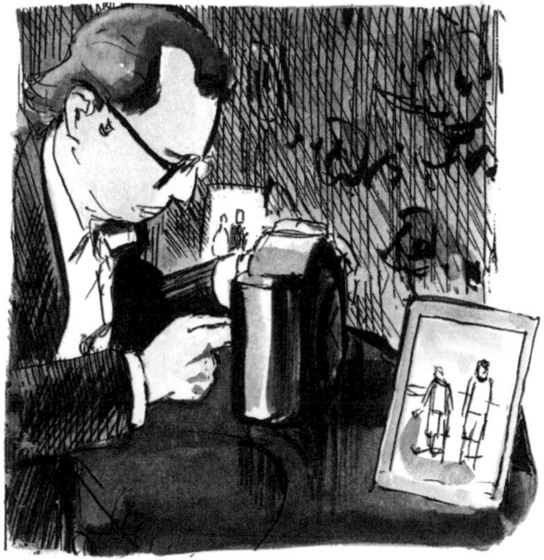

But he never wastes
good material.

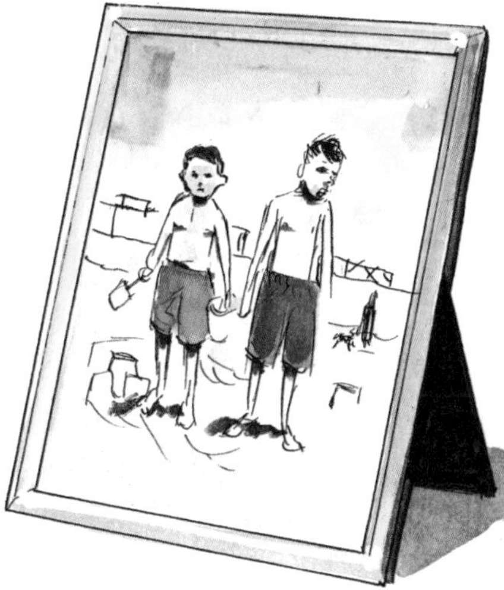

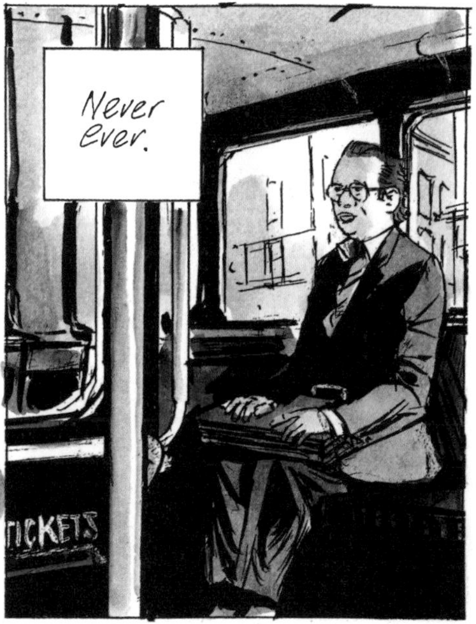
Never
ever.
TICKETS

The playwright returns home to collate the notes he has mentally formed during the day.

As the kettle boils, he thinks he can see the formation of a new idea.

He'll soon begin the first draft.

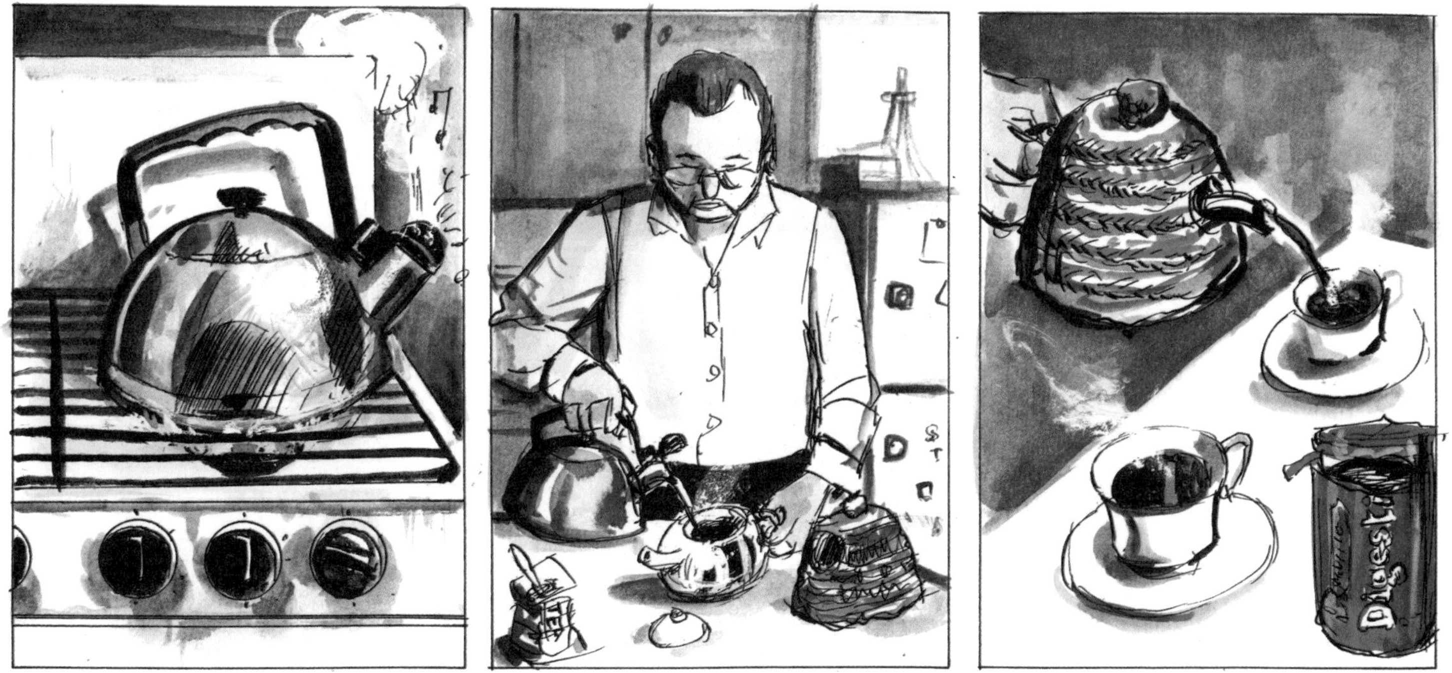

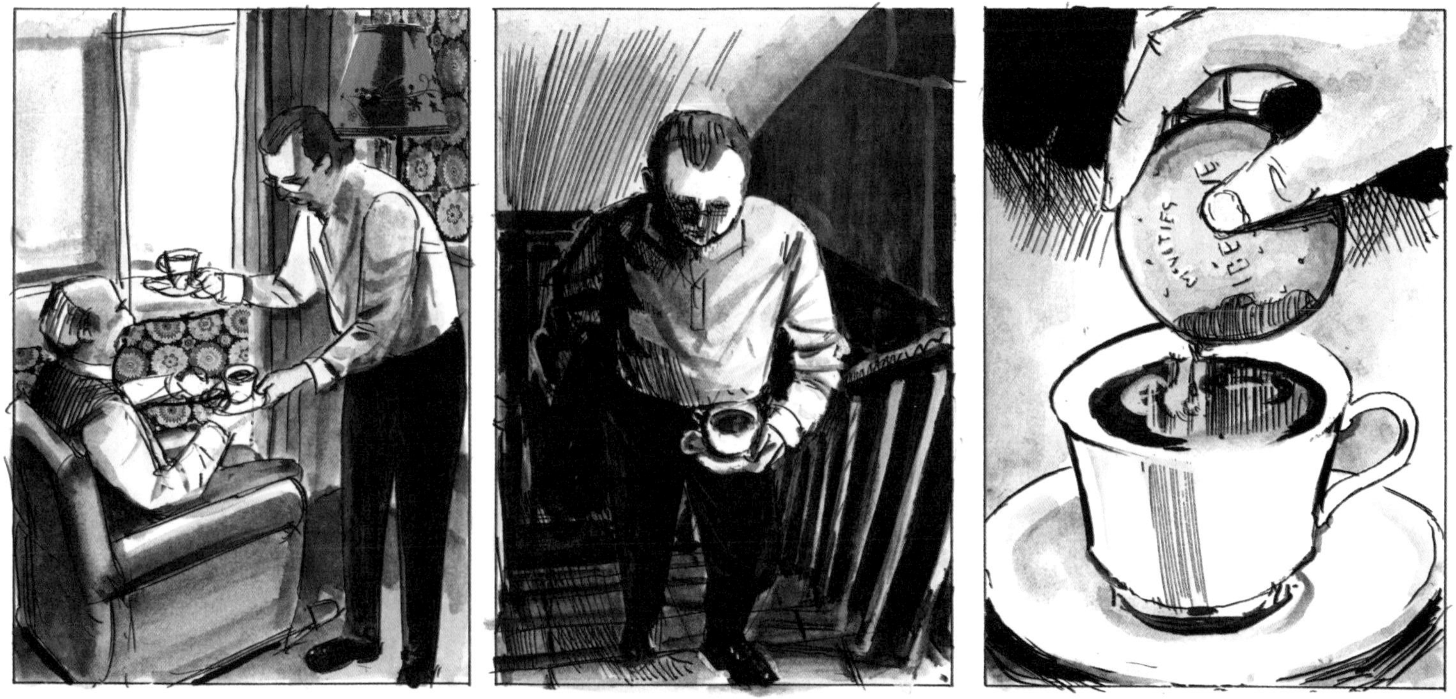
McVITIES

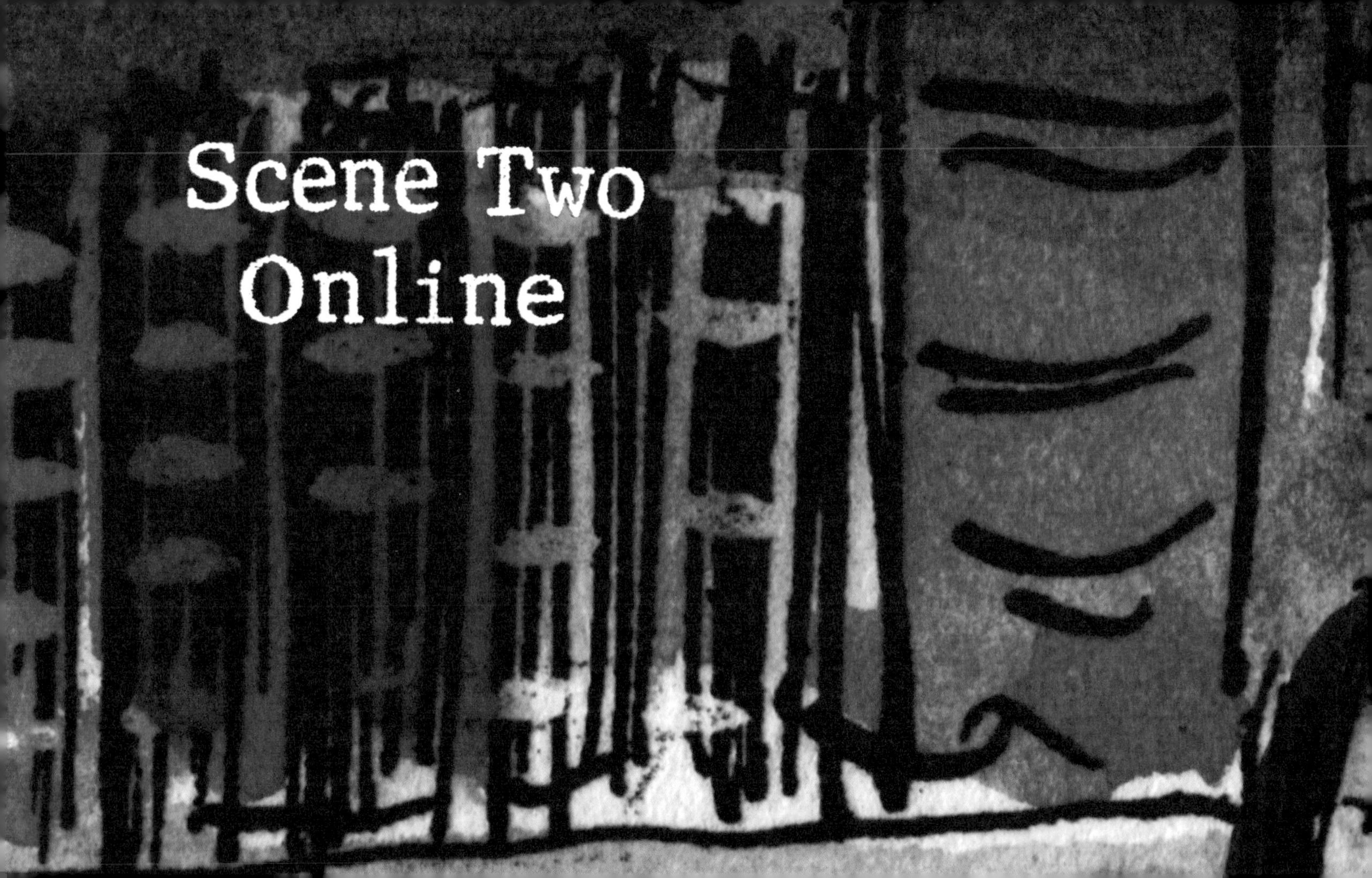
Scene Two
Online

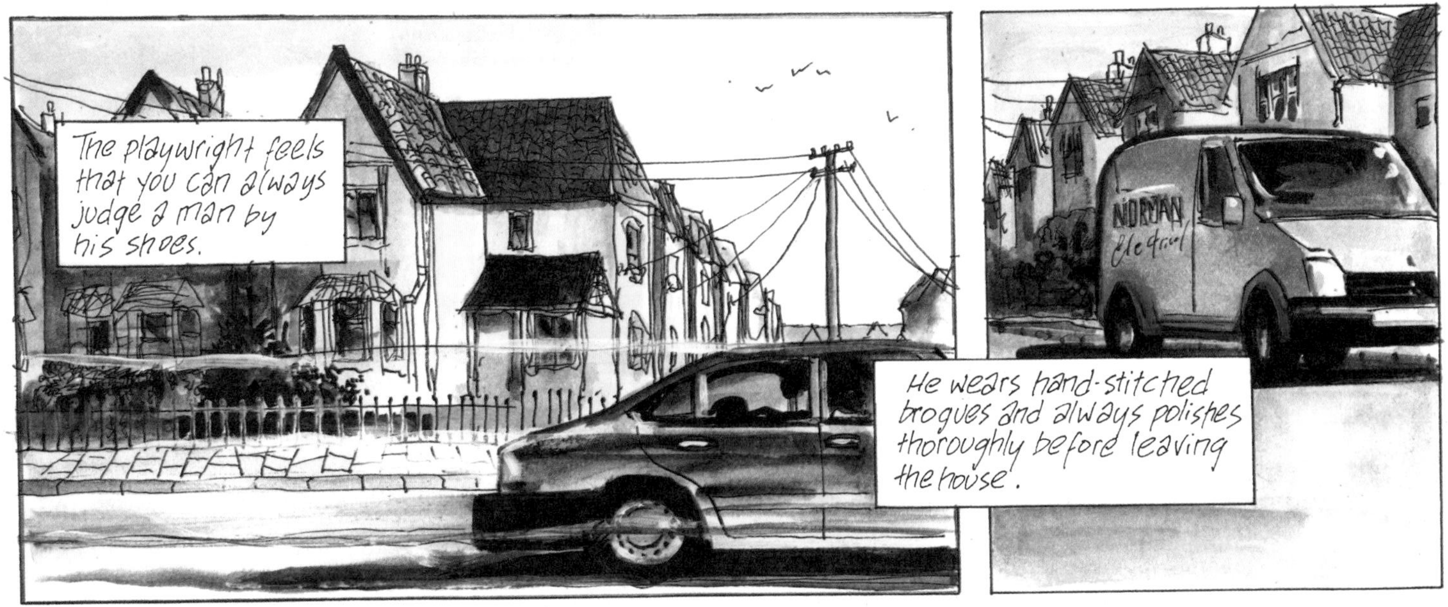
The playwright feels that you can always judge a man by his shoes.
He wears hand-stitched brogues and always polishes thoroughly before leaving the house.
NORMAN

The price of quality footwear has risen greatly in comparison to inflation over the years, but the playwright considers the cost of shabbiness far higher.

Unlike the tradesman who delivers his new personal computer.

Although new to home computing, the playwright is confident that the word processing features will prove useful.

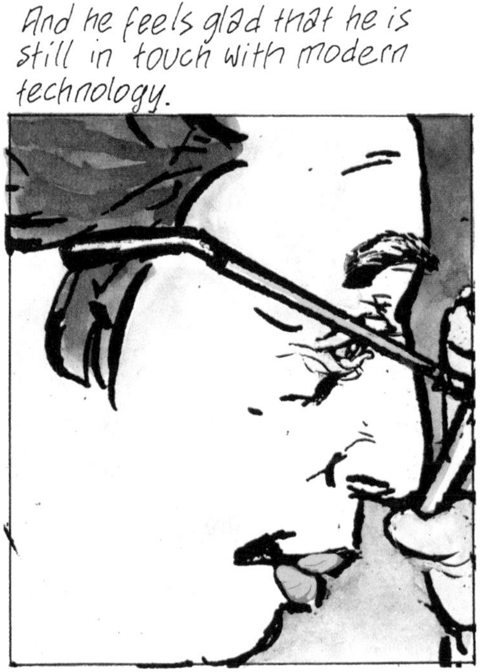
And he feels glad that he is still in touch with modern technology.

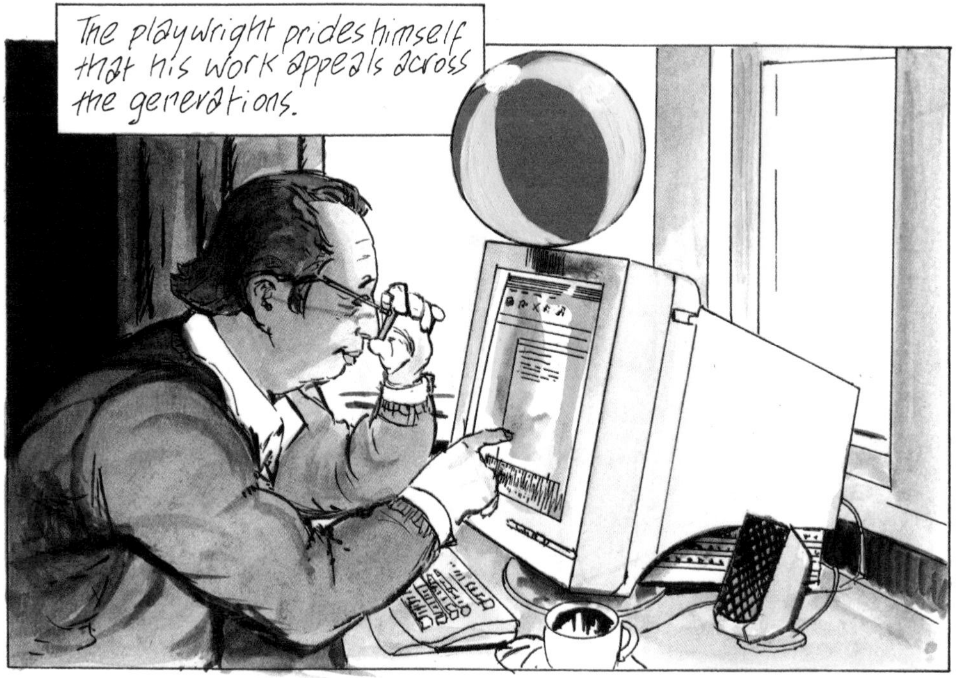
The playwright prides himself that his work appeals across the generations.

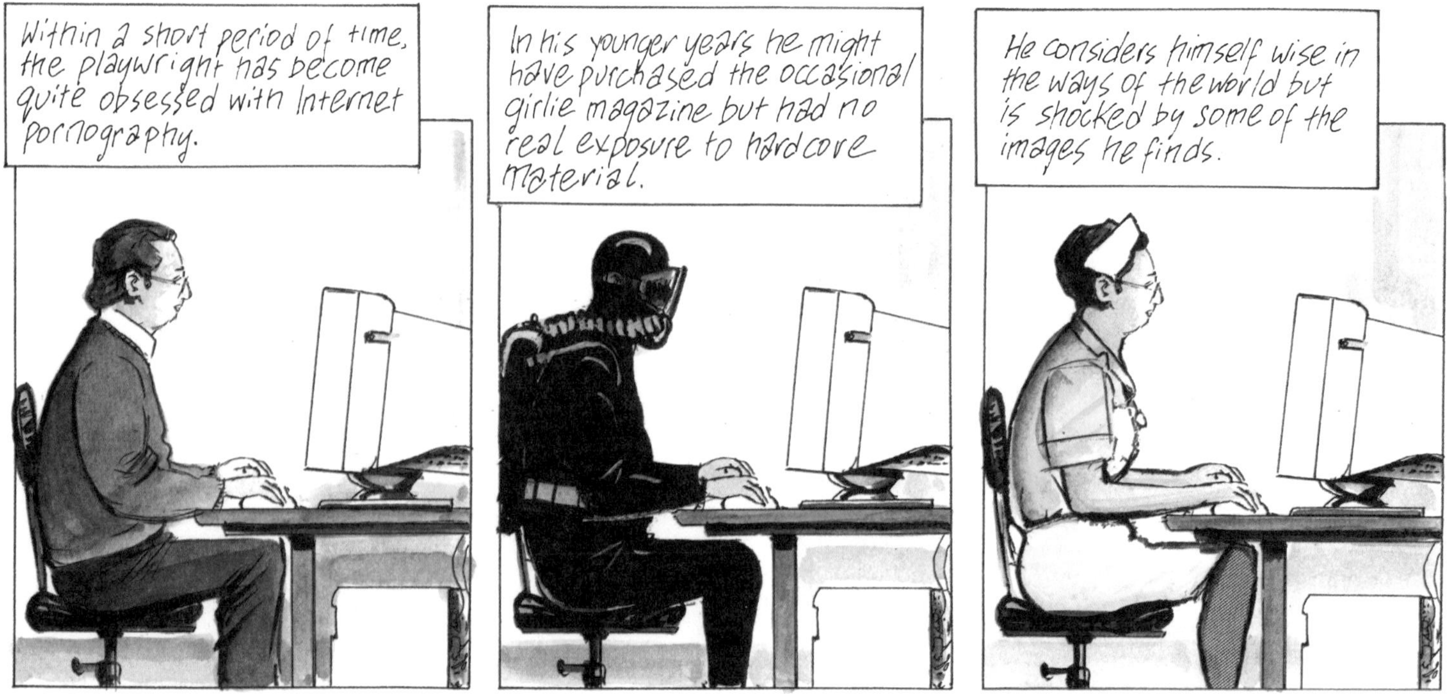
Within a short period of time, the playwright has become quite obsessed with Internet pornography.
In his younger years he might have purchased the occasional girlie magazine but had no real exposure to hardcore material.
He considers himself wise in the ways of the world but is shocked by some of the images he finds.

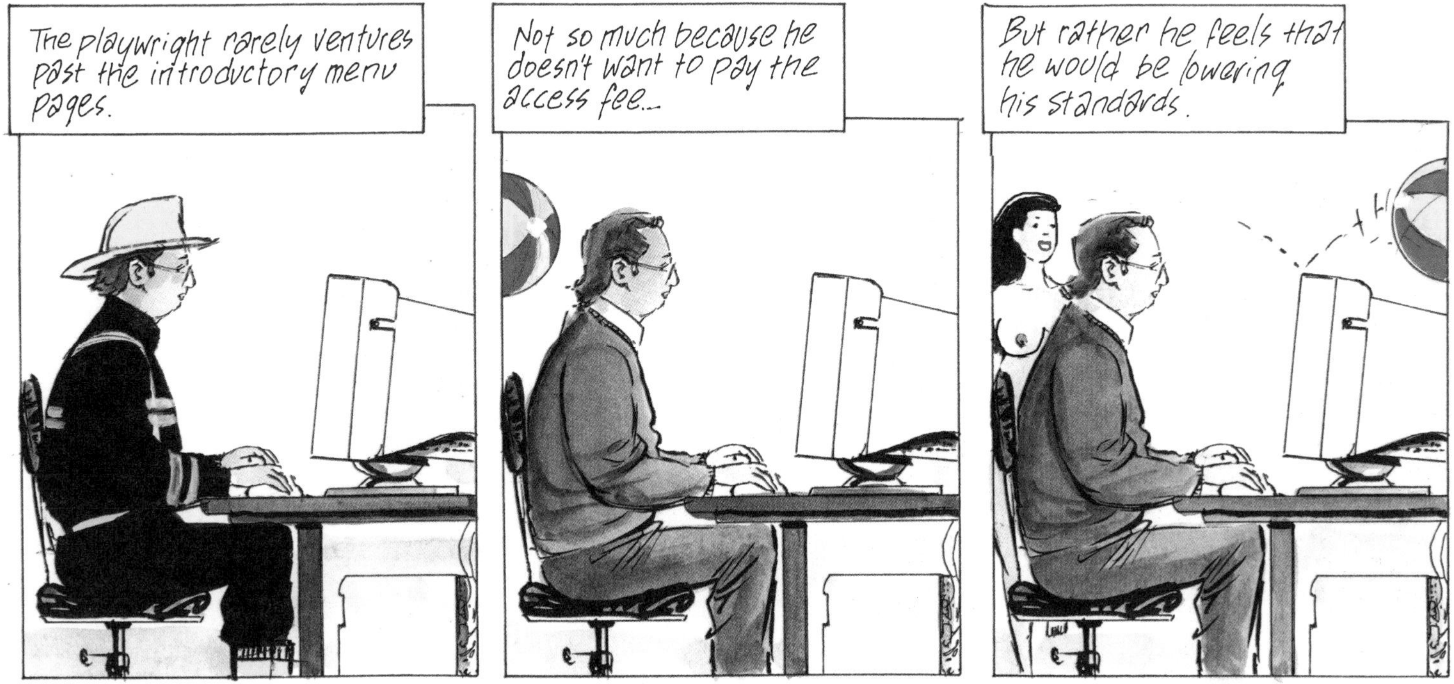

The playwright rarely ventures past the introductory menu pages.
Not so much because he doesn't want to pay the access fee...
But rather he feels that he would be lowering his standards.

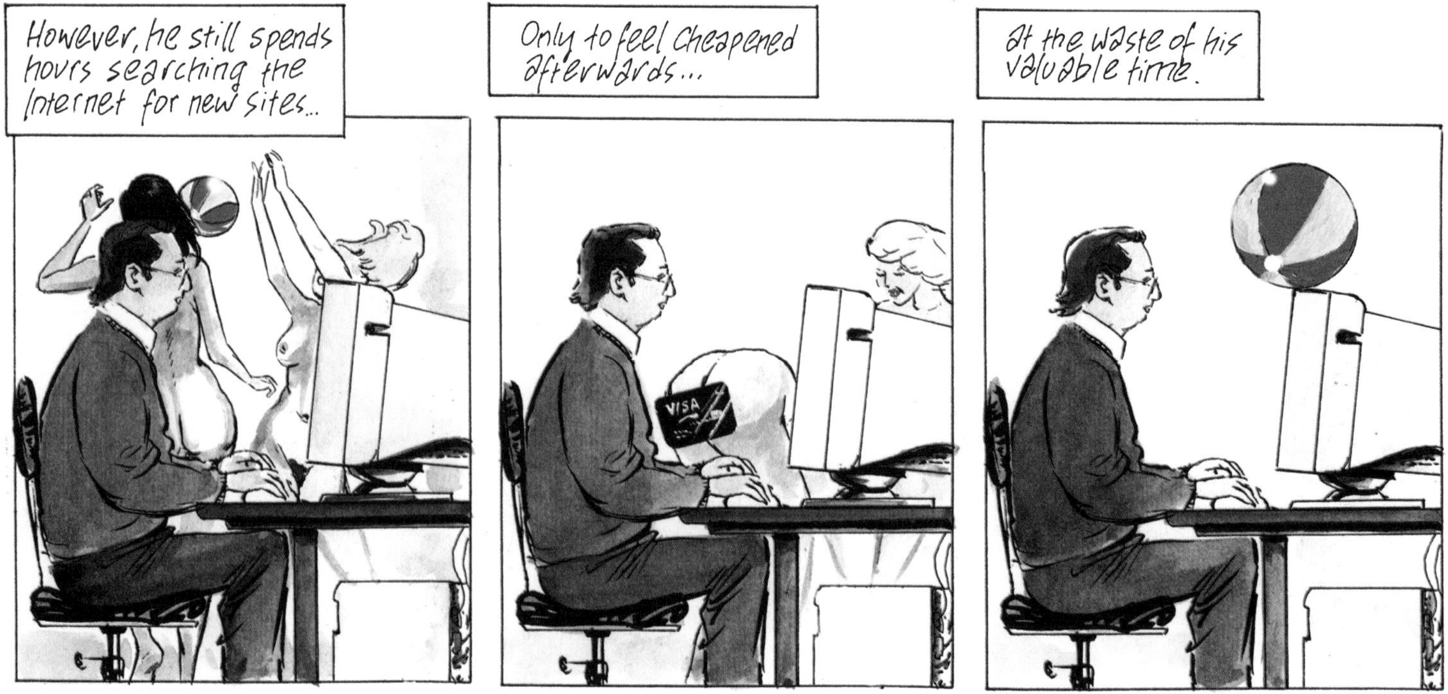
However, he still spends hours searching the Internet for new sites...
Only to feel cheapened afterwards...
VISA
at the waste of his valuable time.

The playwright makes a monthly visit to his agent's office.

His success over the years has made him an important client, and he feels that an occasional lunch is the least he deserves.

33

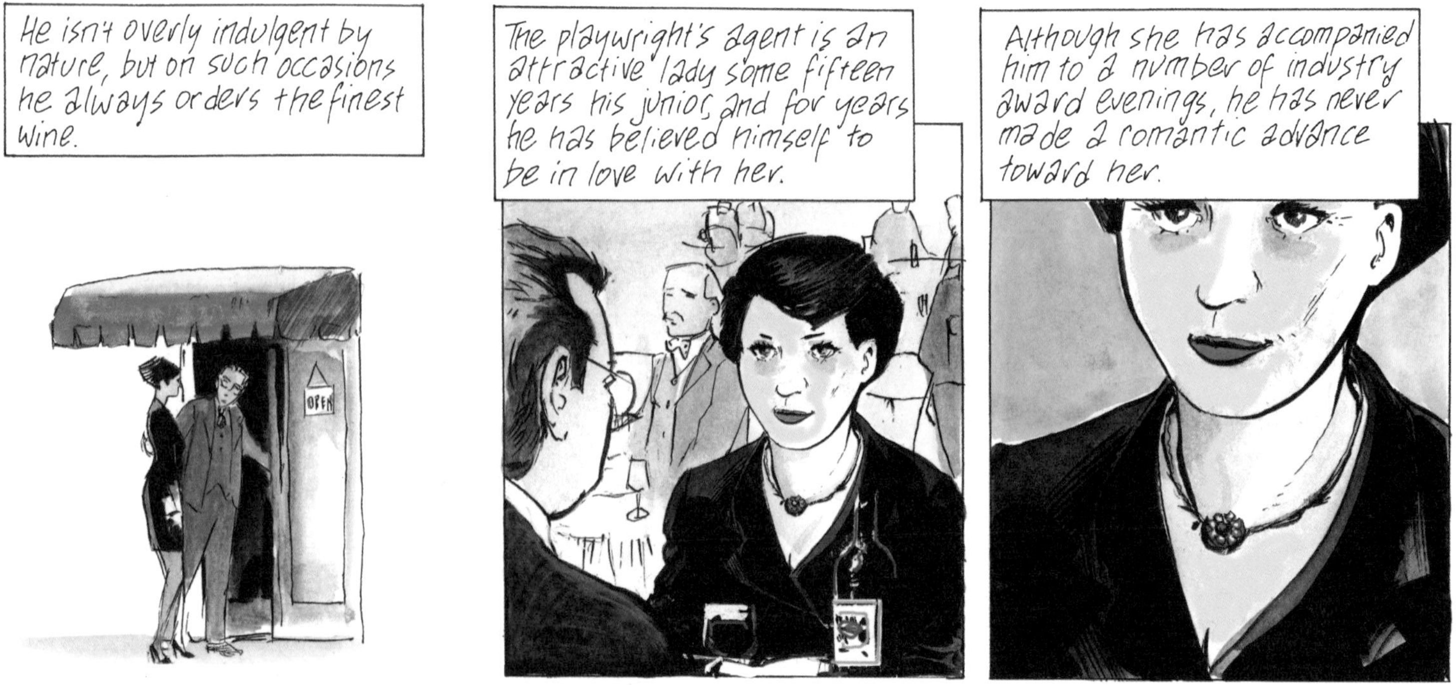
He isn't overly indulgent by nature, but on such occasions he always orders the finest wine.
OPEN
The playwright's agent is an attractive lady some fifteen years his junior, and for years he has believed himself to be in love with her.
Although she has accompanied him to a number of industry award evenings, he has never made a romantic advance toward her.

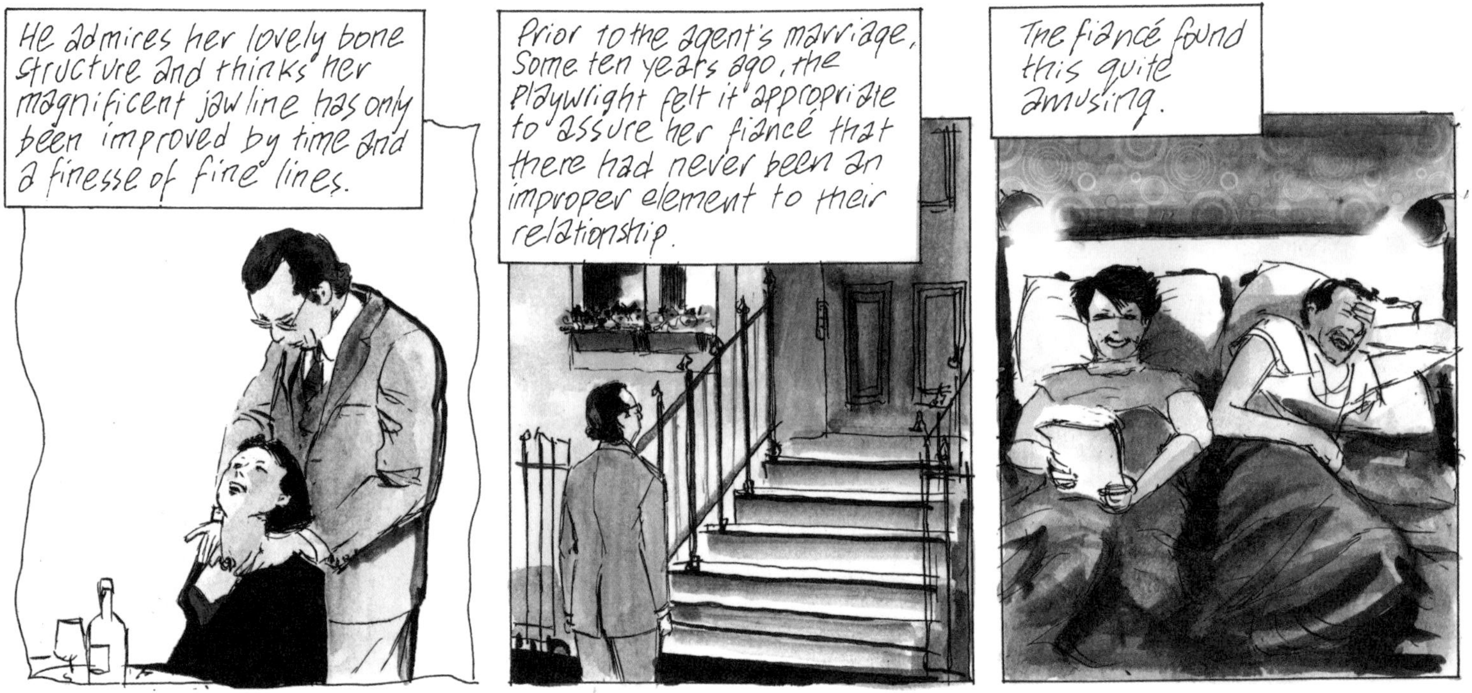
He admires her lovely bone structure and thinks her magnificent jawline has only been improved by time and a finesse of fine lines.
Prior to the agent's marriage, some ten years ago, the playwright felt it appropriate to assure her fiancé that there had never been an improper element to their relationship.
The fiancé found this quite amusing.

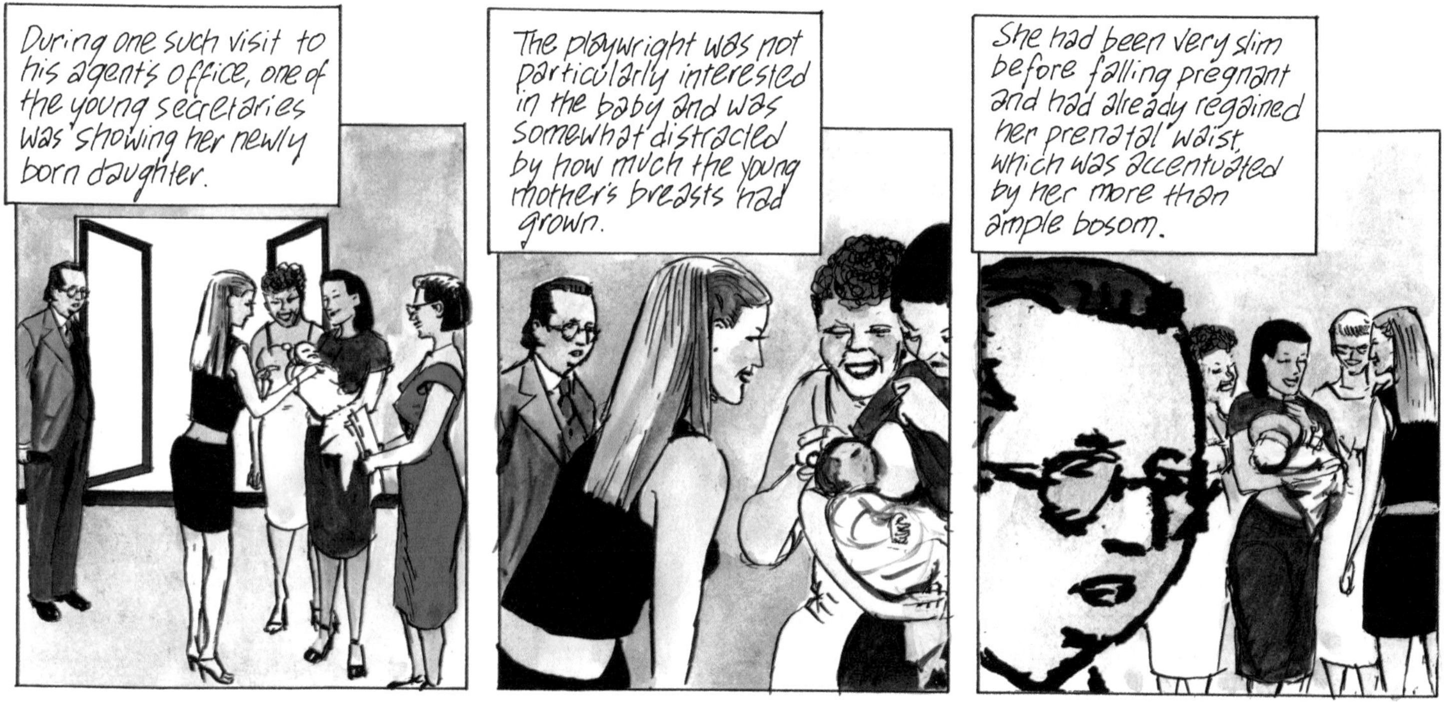
During one such visit to his agent's office, one of the young secretaries was showing her newly born daughter.
The playwright was not particularly interested in the baby and was somewhat distracted by how much the young mother's breasts had grown.
She had been very slim before falling pregnant and had already regained her prenatal waist, which was accentuated by her more than ample bosom.

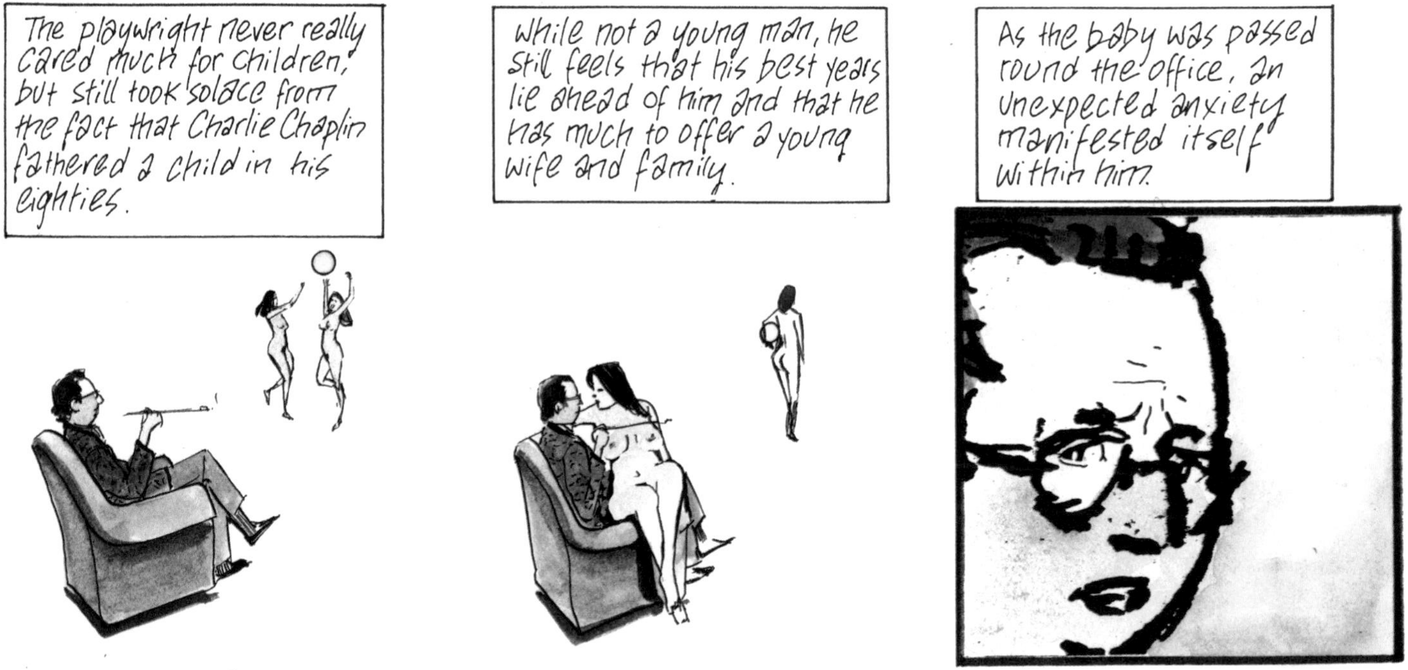
The playwright never really cared much for children, but still took solace from the fact that Charlie Chaplin fathered a child in his eighties.
While not a young man, he still feels that his best years lie ahead of him and that he has much to offer a young wife and family.
As the baby was passed round the office, an unexpected anxiety manifested itself within him.

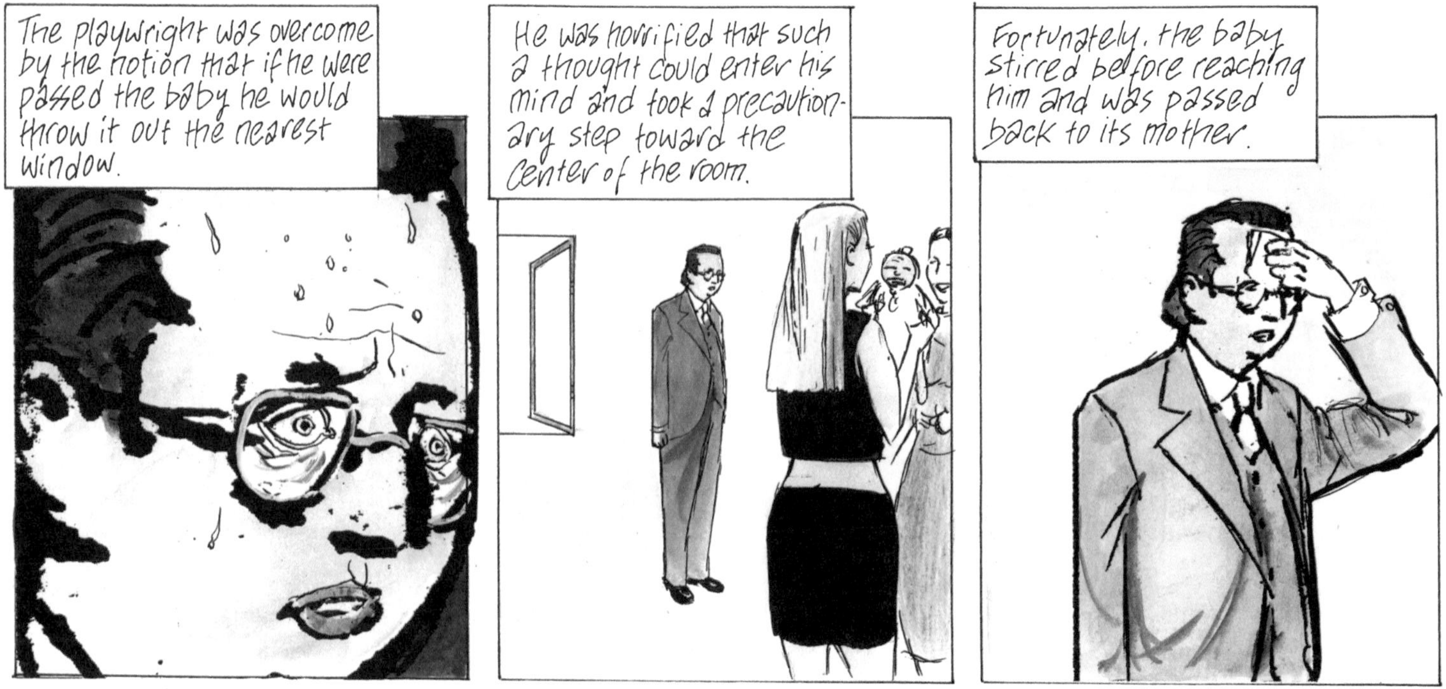
The playwright was overcome by the notion that if he were passed the baby he would throw it out the nearest window.
He was horrified that such a thought could enter his mind and took a precautionary step toward the center of the room.
Fortunately, the baby stirred before reaching him and was passed back to its mother.

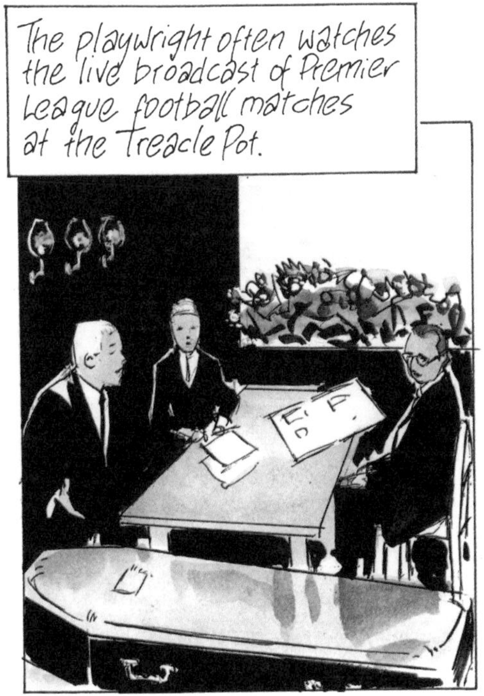
The playwright often watches the live broadcast of Premier League football matches at the Treacle Pot.

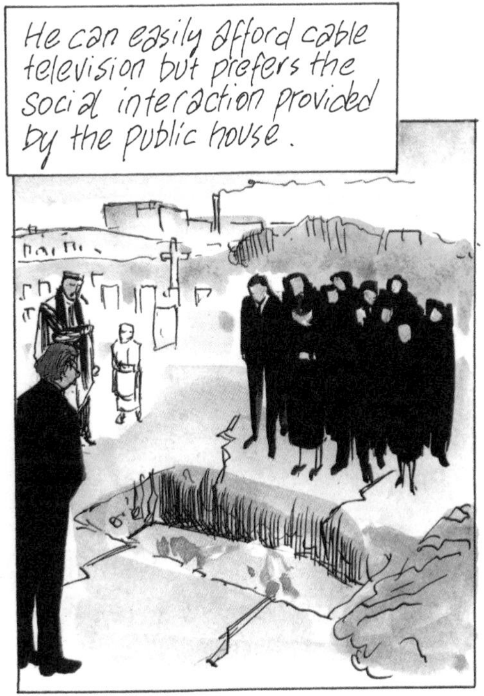
He can easily afford cable television but prefers the social interaction provided by the public house.

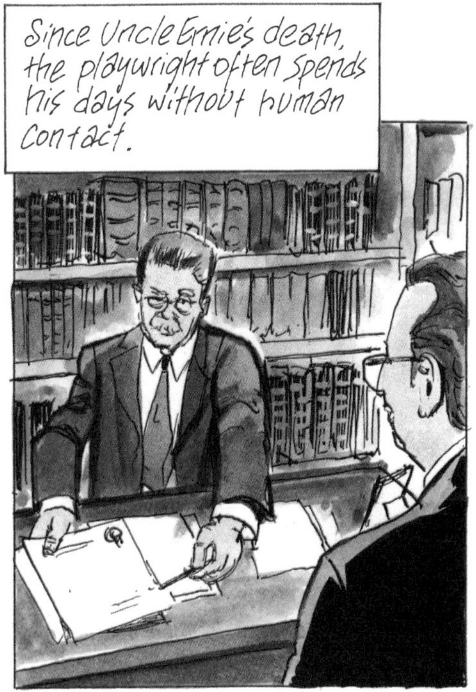
Since Uncle Ernie's death, the playwright often spends his days without human contact.

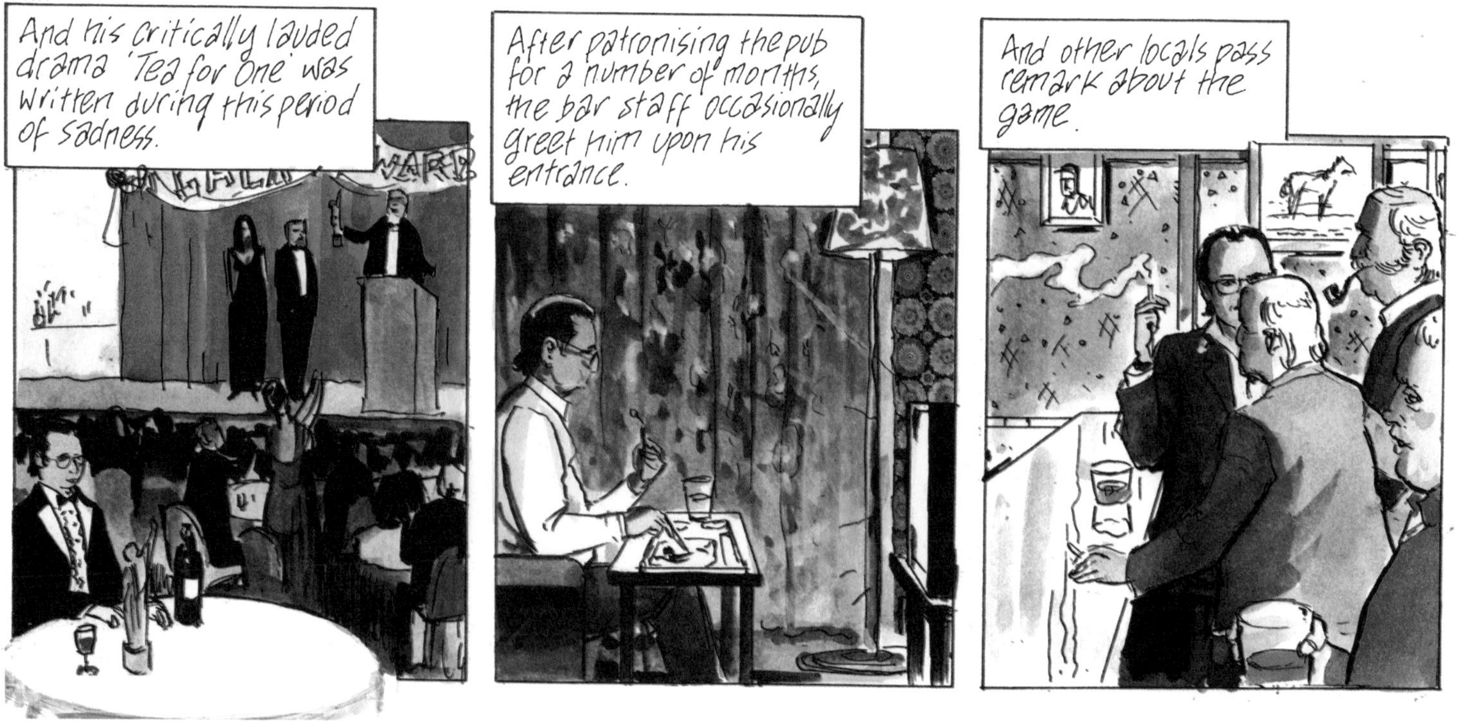
And his critically lauded drama 'Tea for One' was written during this period of sadness.
After patronising the pub for a number of months, the bar staff occasionally greet him upon his entrance.
And other locals pass remark about the game.

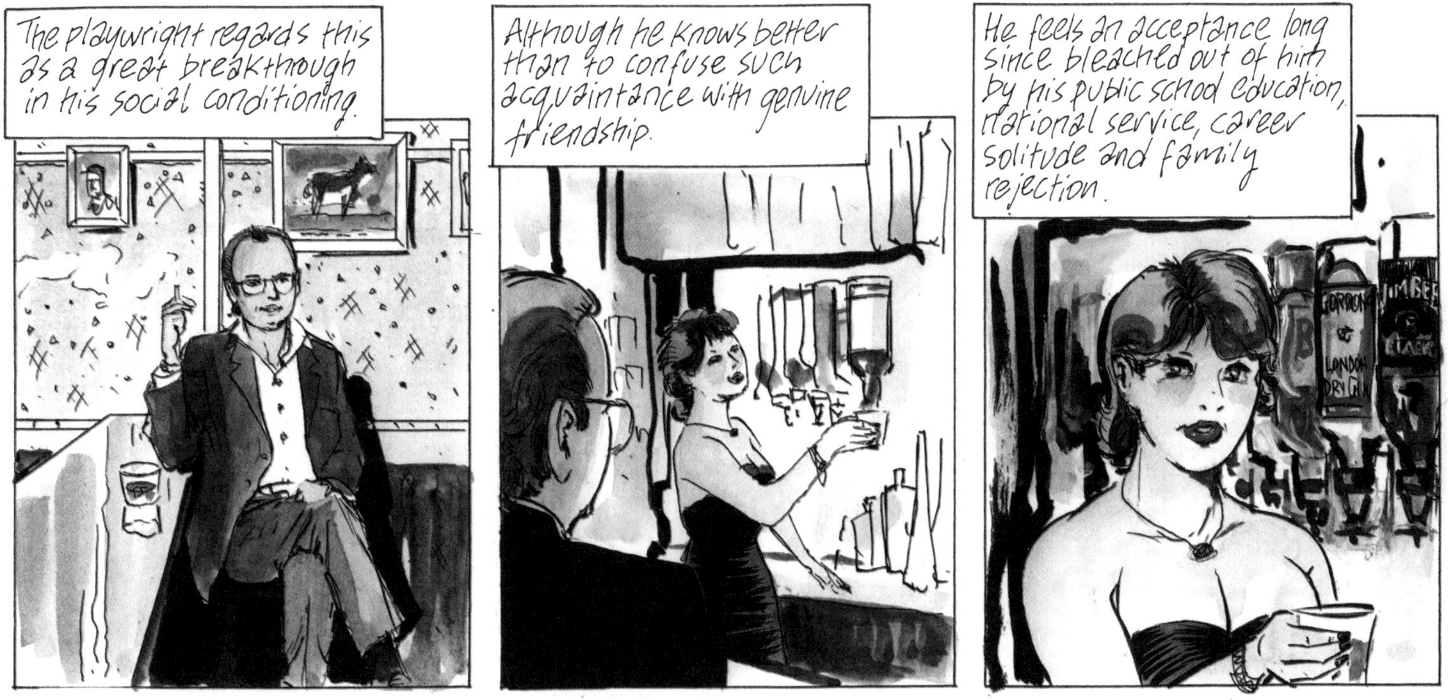
The playwright regards this as a great breakthrough in his social conditioning.
Although he knows better than to confuse such acquaintance with genuine friendship.
He feels an acceptance long since bleached out of him by his public school education, national service, career solitude and family rejection.

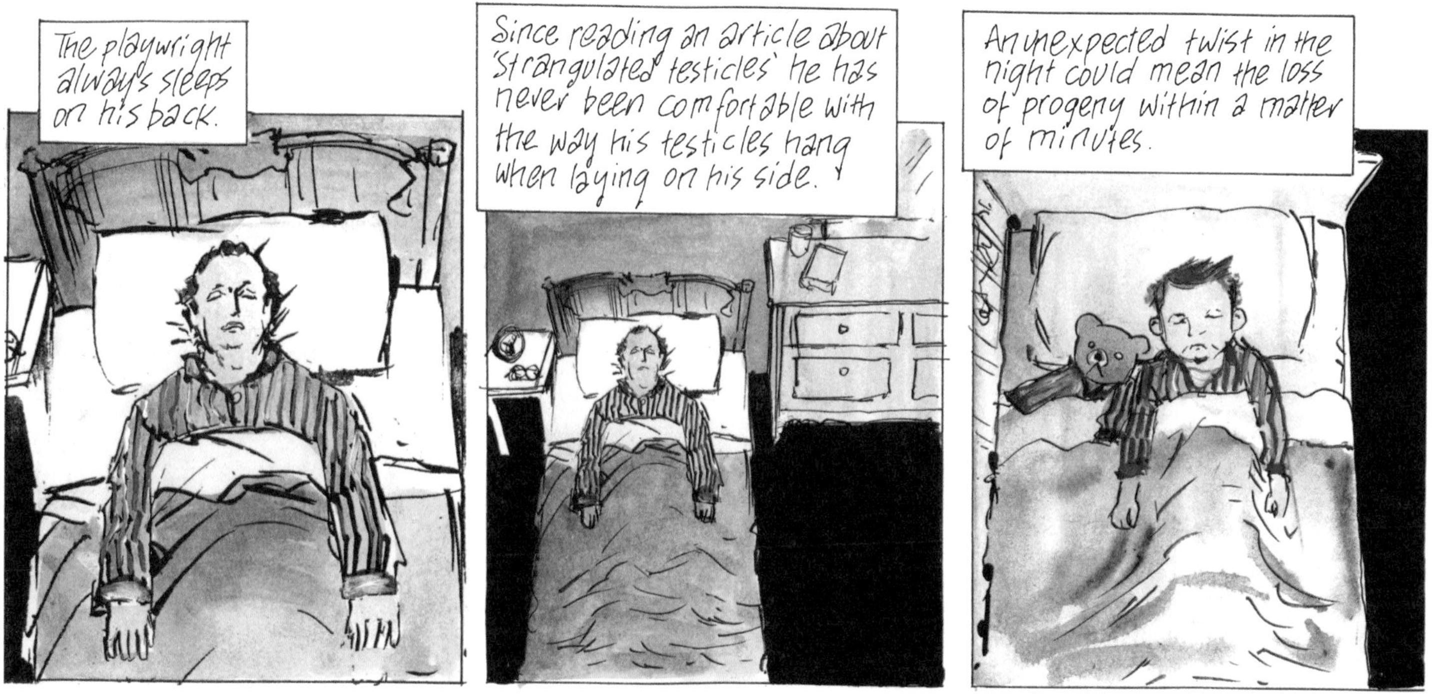
The playwright always sleeps on his back.
Since reading an article about 'Strangulated testicles' he has never been comfortable with the way his testicles hang when laying on his side.
An unexpected twist in the night could mean the loss of progeny within a matter of minutes.

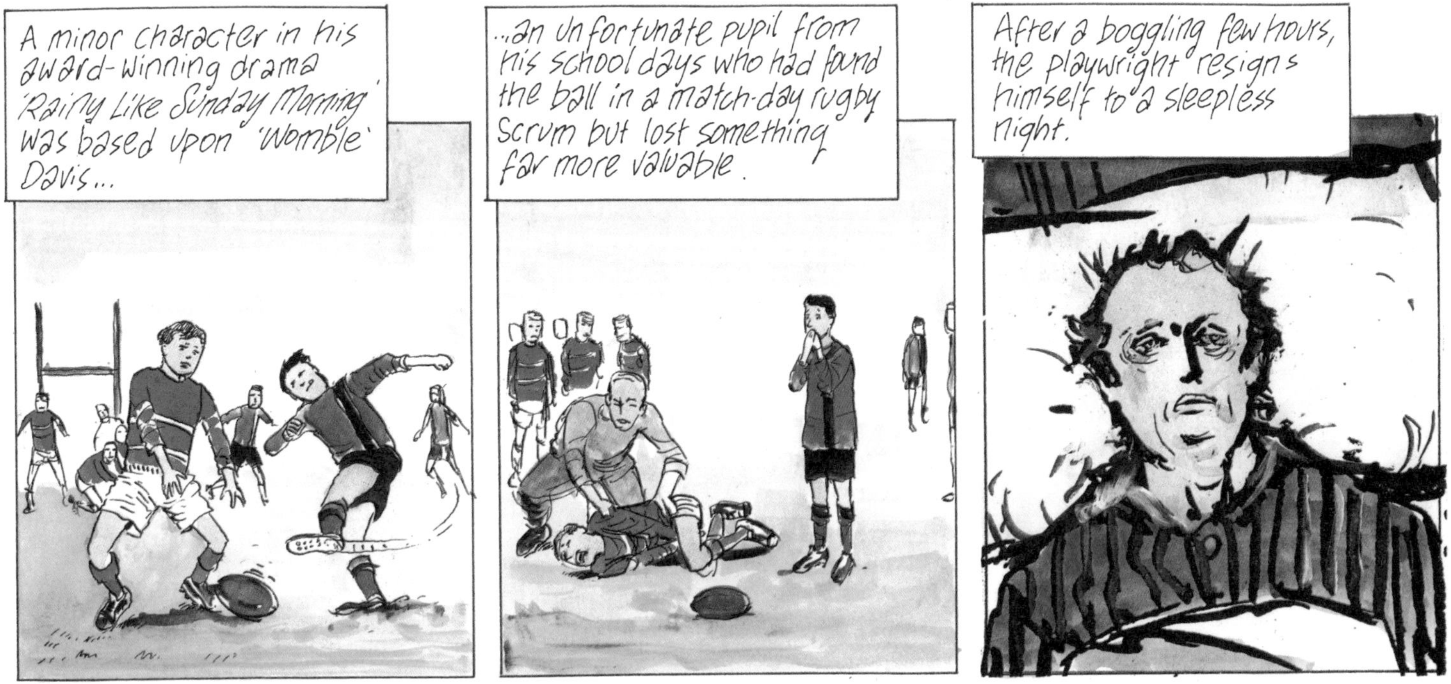
A minor character in his award-winning drama 'Rainy Like Sunday Morning' was based upon 'Womble' Davis...
...an unfortunate pupil from his school days who had found the ball in a match-day rugby scrum but lost something far more valuable.
After a boggling few hours, the playwright resigns himself to a sleepless night.

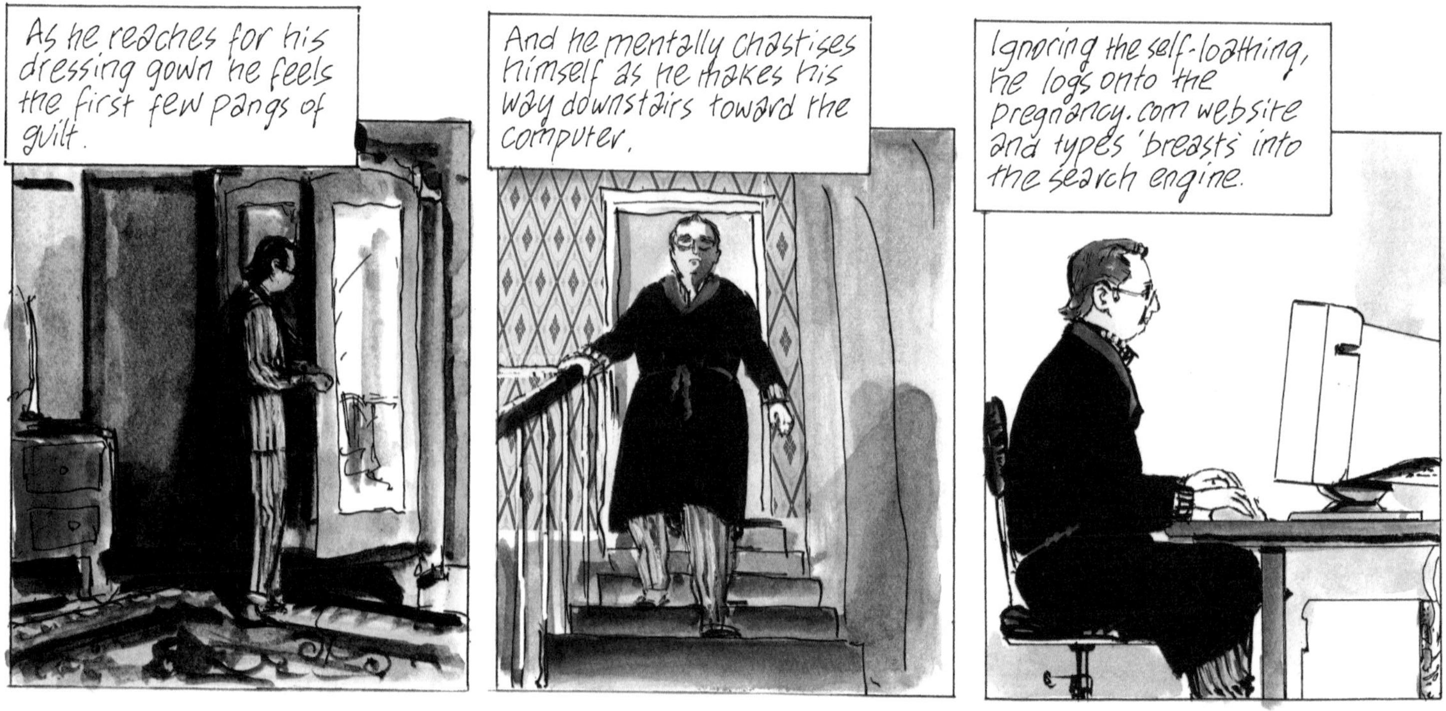
As he reaches for his dressing gown he feels the first few pangs of guilt.
And he mentally chastises himself as he makes his way downstairs toward the computer.
Ignoring the self-loathing, he logs onto the pregnancy.com website and types 'breasts' into the search engine.

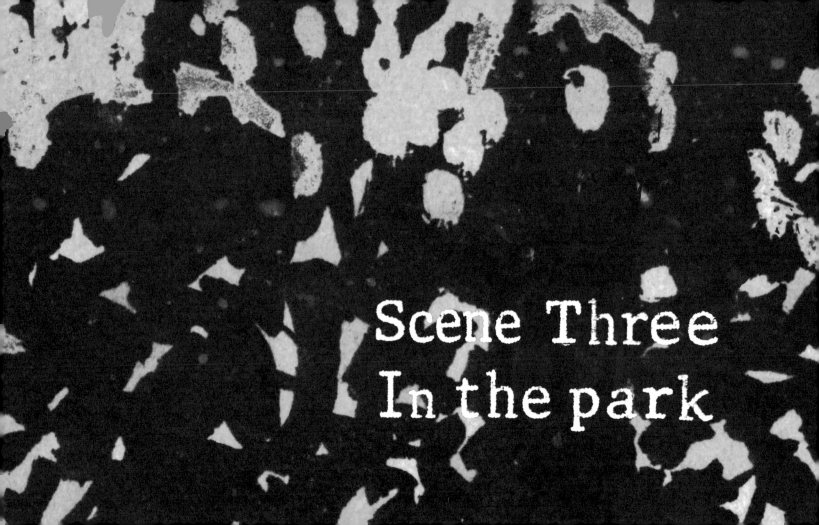

Scene Three
In the park

The playwright rather enjoys a quiet moment in the park.

It's a good place to mentally sort his ideas and is often frequented by pretty young ladies.

He once saw a pigeon defecate on to a businessman's shoulder.

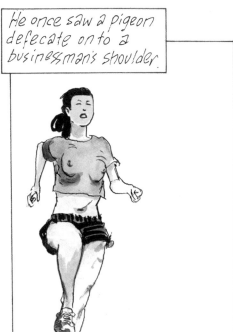

It strikes him as absurd that such an event is often considered lucky.

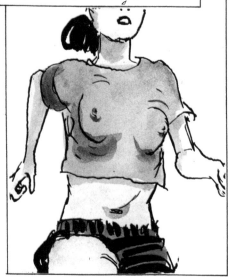

Surely the luck lies with passers by who, statistically, are far less likely to be similarly soiled at that precise moment.

In the same way, the playwright always derives an almost perverse sense of relief whenever he receives news that an old friend has developed prostate cancer.

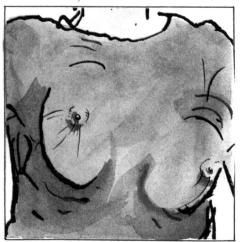

Because statistically, he reasons such news significantly reduces the danger of him being similarly afflicted.

And to be honest, at his age his prostate needs all the statistical support he can muster.

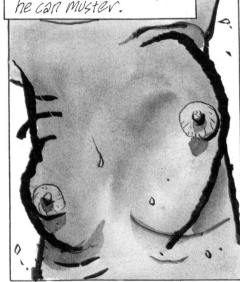

49

Scene Four
At school

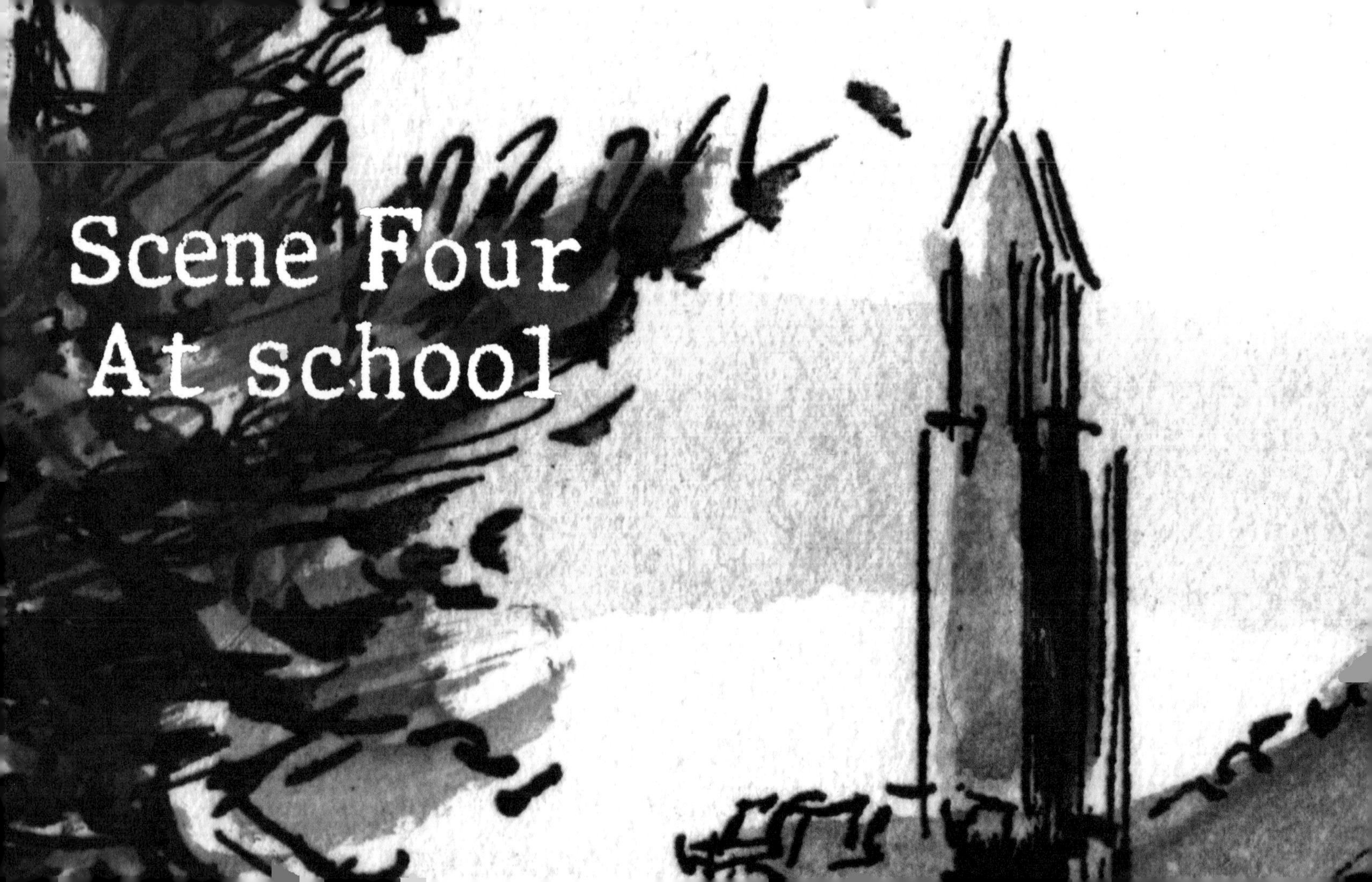

The playwright spends a ridiculous amount of time cashing some Premium Bonds at his local Post Office.

The delay originated with the counter clerk's reluctance to admit her failing eyesight.

He assumes that vanity is playing a role, which seems odd, considering the woman's age, obesity and fashion sense.

The playwright is rarely a victim to vanity, although he was somewhat alarmed when his hairline began to fail while still in his early thirties.

However, he considered it absurd to fret excessively over an uncontrollable imperfection when he was riddled with a number of other aberrations.

52

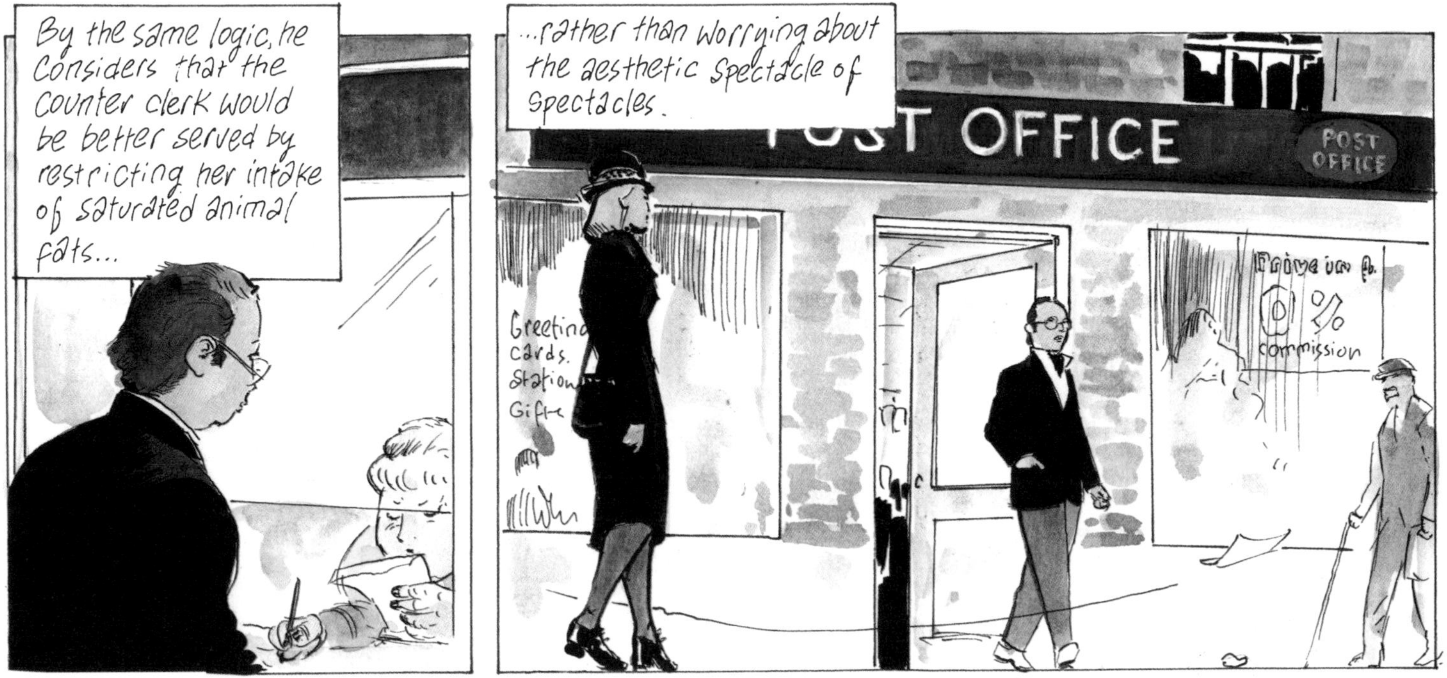
By the same logic, he considers that the counter clerk would be better served by restricting her intake of saturated animal fats...
...rather than worrying about the aesthetic spectacle of spectacles.
POST OFFICE
POST OFFICE
Greeting cards.
10%
commission

The playwright had been a clever child.

A high pass at the eleven-plus examination had secured a scholarship for a nearby school of fine repute.

The playwright's retarded older brother required constant attention and so his family had opted for him to board at the school.

He immediately struggled with the sudden immersion in such a strict and loveless environment.

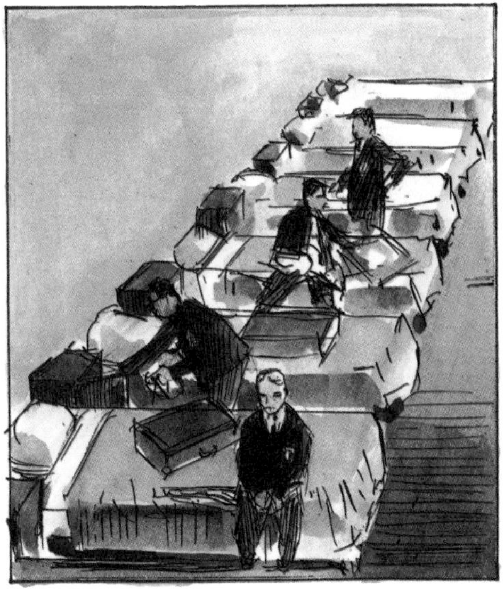

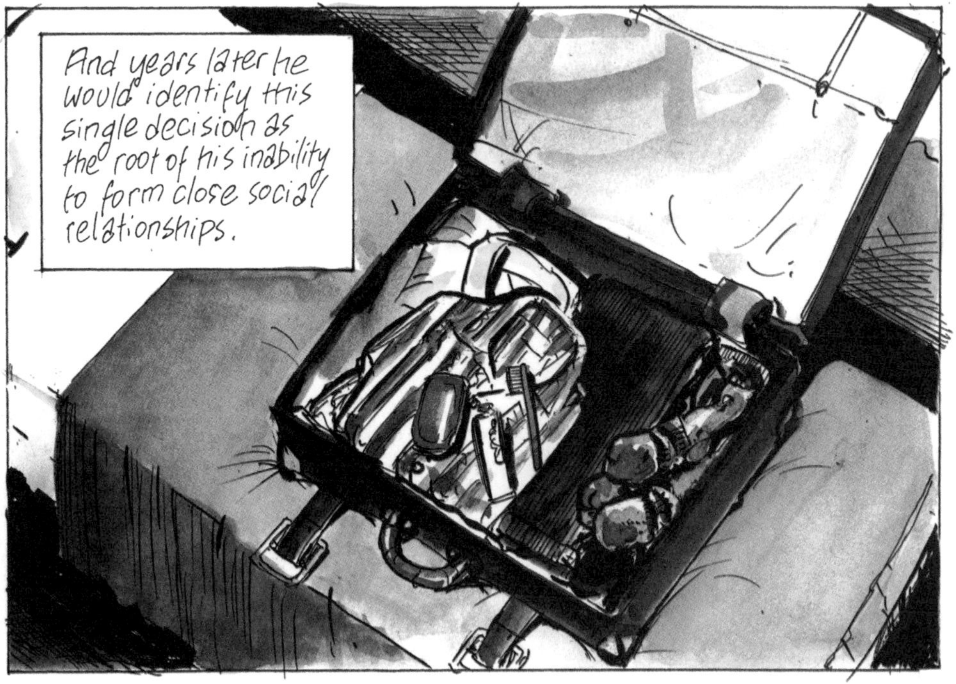
And years later he would identify this single decision as the root of his inability to form close social relationships.

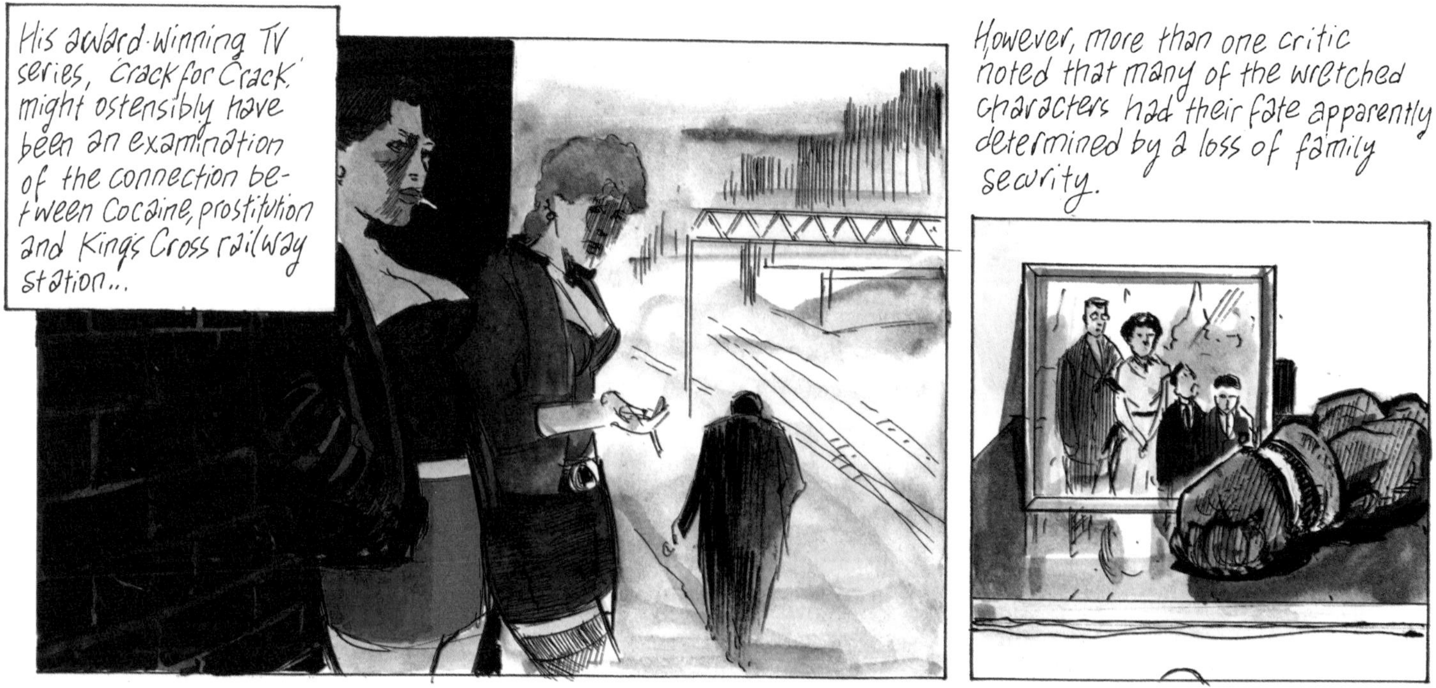
His award-winning TV series, 'Crack for Crack' might ostensibly have been an examination of the connection between Cocaine, prostitution and Kings Cross railway station...
However, more than one critic noted that many of the wretched characters had their fate apparently determined by a loss of family security.

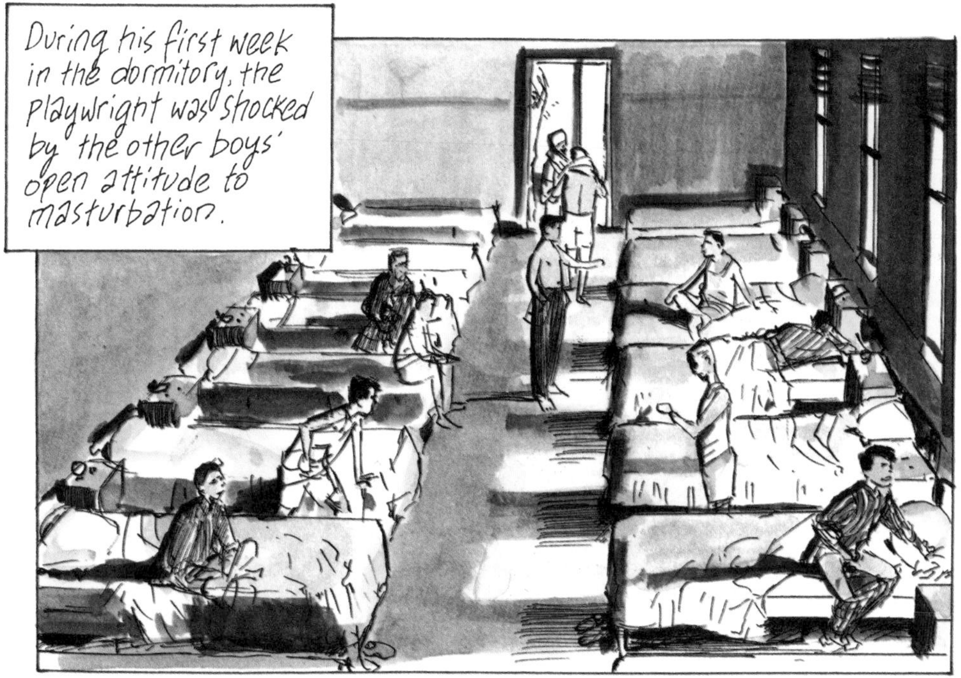
During his first week in the dormitory, the playwright was shocked by the other boys' open attitude to masturbation.

For some time he had suspected that he was not isolated in his pleasure of the palm. However, at such a fragile age, he could imagine nothing worse than honesty.

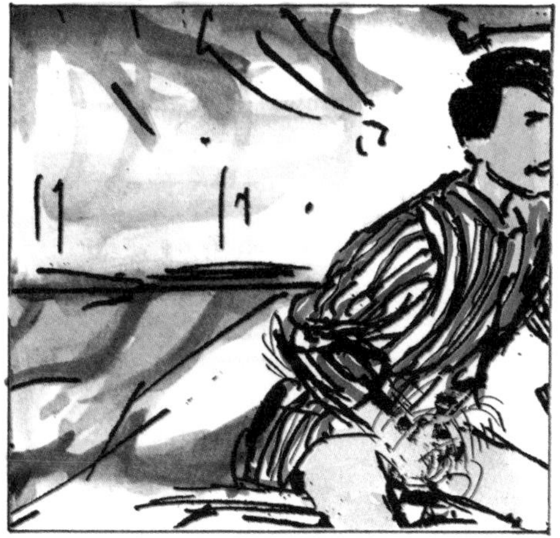

The playwright was also shocked by the maturity of the older boys.

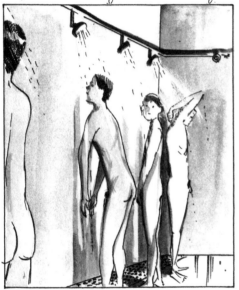

His was not a family at ease with the naked body.

And beyond the occasional glimpse of his brother, he had no basis upon which to form comparison.

The playwright's own sexual immaturity often made him the unfortunate target of the prefect's bullying.

And were it not for the persistent bedwetting of the unfortunately named Pryke...

...his first few terms might have proven unbearable.

59

The playwright's bed was situated next to that of a young lad who couldn't be classified as an obsessive self-abuser...

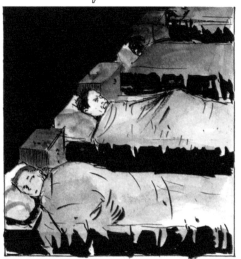

...but who would, on random occasions, awake in the small hours and frantically pleasure himself, with little regard for the other boys.

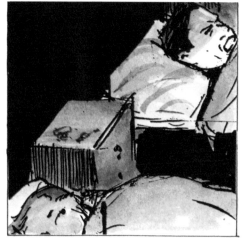

The playwright learned that, on such occasions, his classmate had slept awkwardly upon his arm and awoken with it completely numbed.

His technique was to finish himself off before the onset of pins-and-needles.

This technique became popular within the dormitory and was known as "greeting the stranger".

The playwright adopted the practice himself.

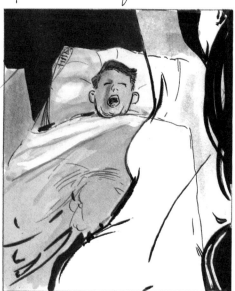

In fact, he came to consider it one of the few invaluable lessons learned during this period of schooling.

In later life, he would deliberately attempt to 'beckon the stranger' by purposely sleeping on his right hand...

...such that the stranger eventually became no stranger at all.

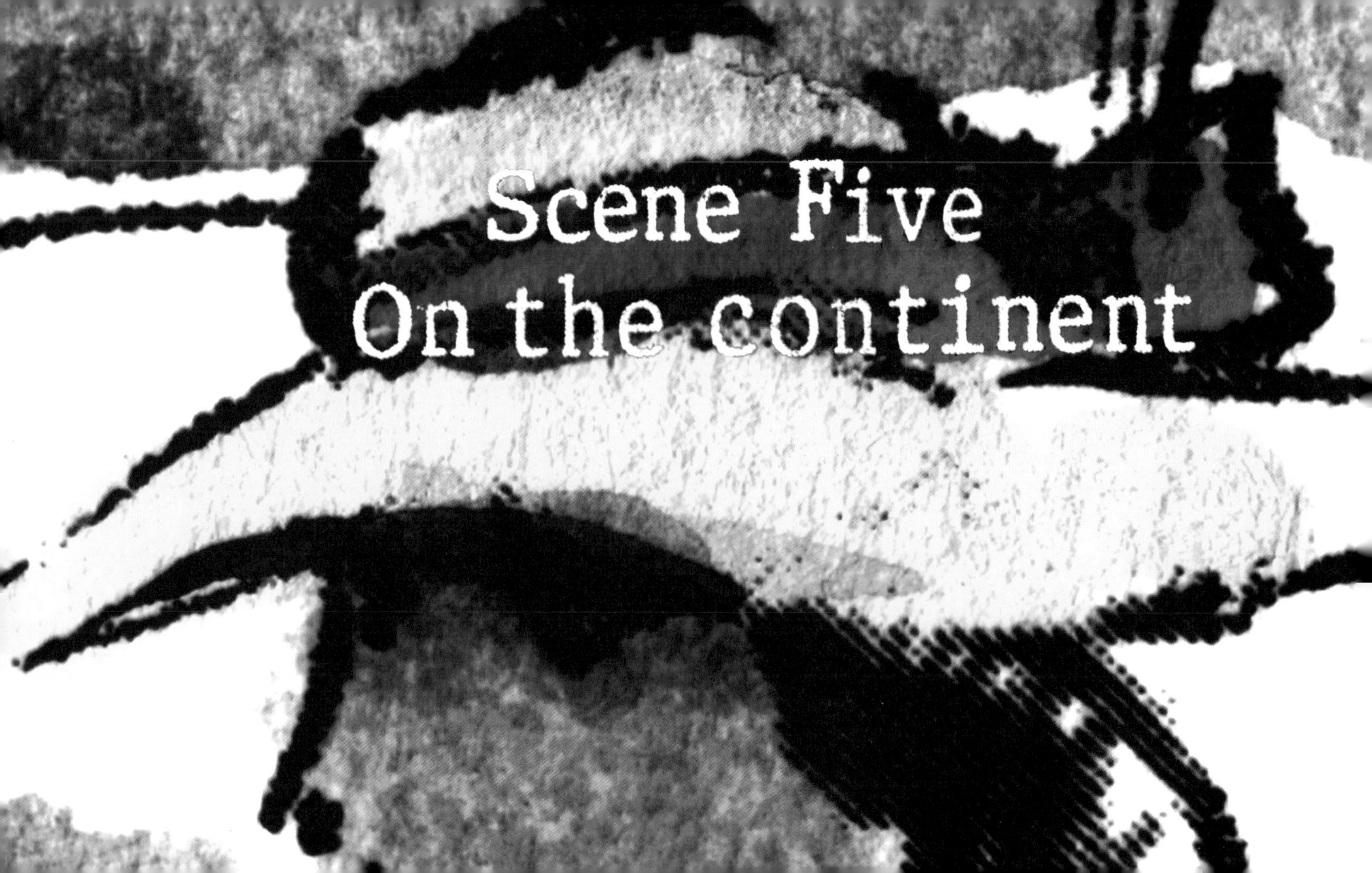
Scene Five
On the continent

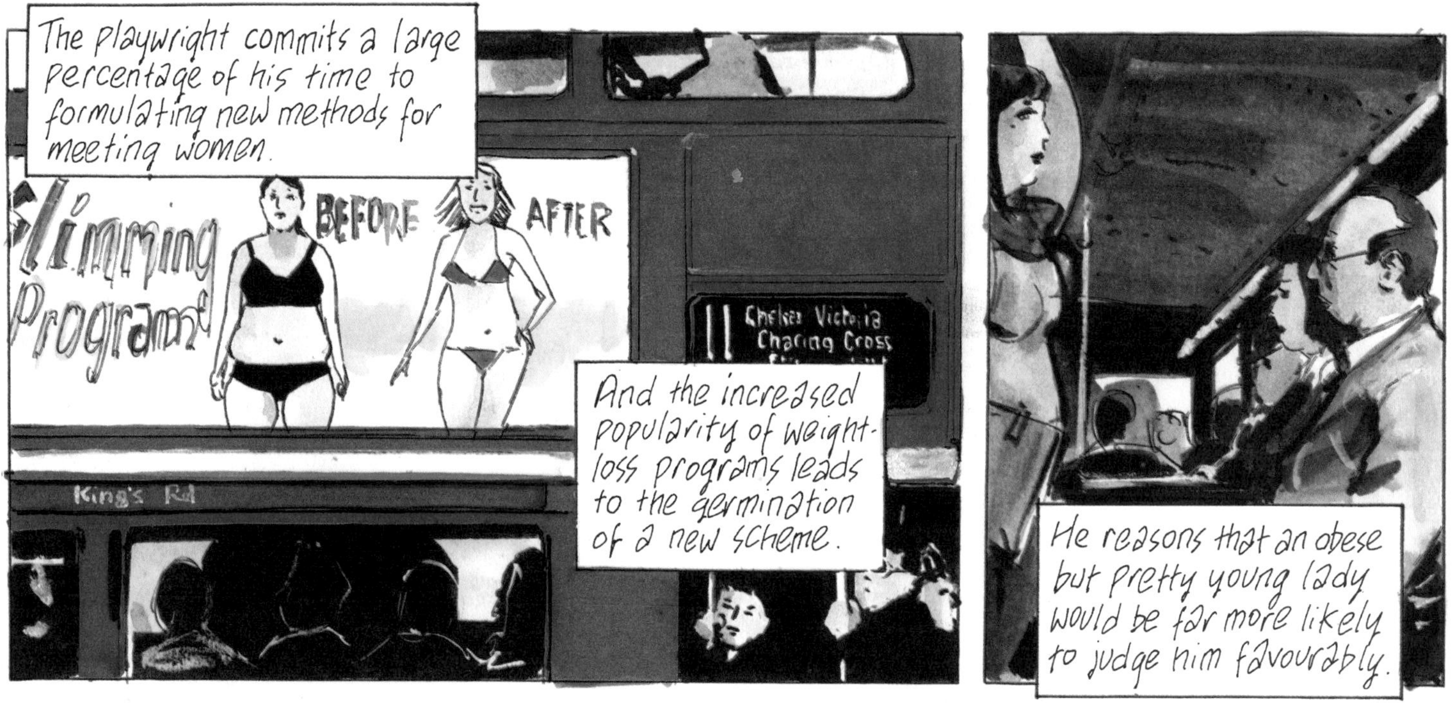
The playwright commits a large percentage of his time to formulating new methods for meeting women.
BEFORE
AFTER
Chelsea Victoria
Charing Cross
King's Rd
And the increased popularity of weight-loss programs leads to the germination of a new scheme.
He reasons that an obese but pretty young lady would be far more likely to judge him favourably.

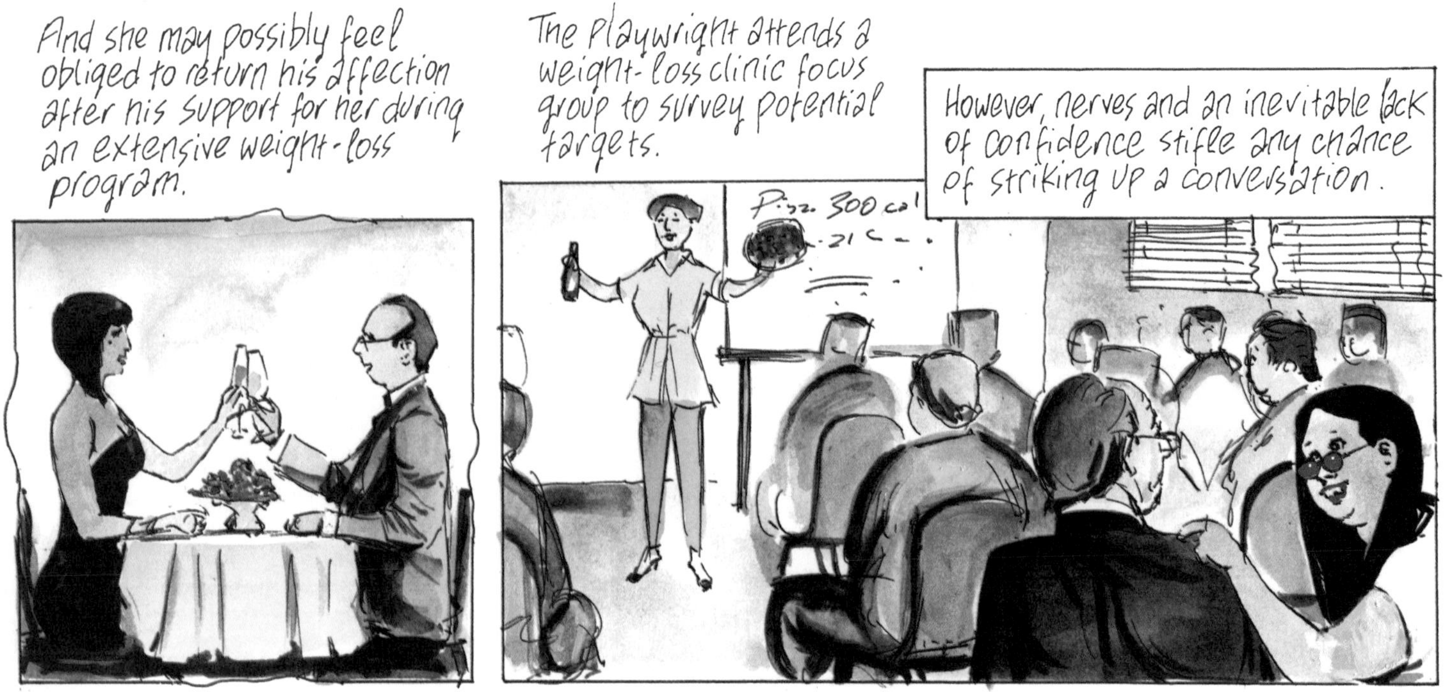
And she may possibly feel obliged to return his affection after his support for her during an extensive weight-loss program.
The Playwright attends a weight-loss clinic focus group to survey potential targets.
However, nerves and an inevitable lack of confidence stifle any chance of striking up a conversation.

Ironically, the playwright soon becomes concerned with his own physique.

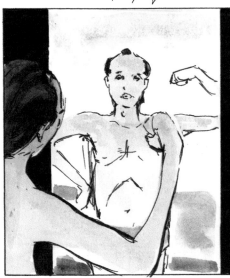

He is by no means obese...

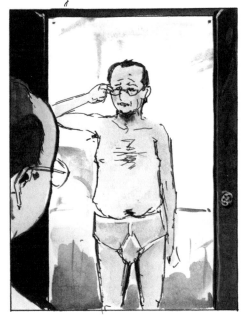

but is definitely somewhat relaxed around the middle.

67

He is alarmingly conscious that some potential young wife... might expect an illuminated room... during conjugal relations.

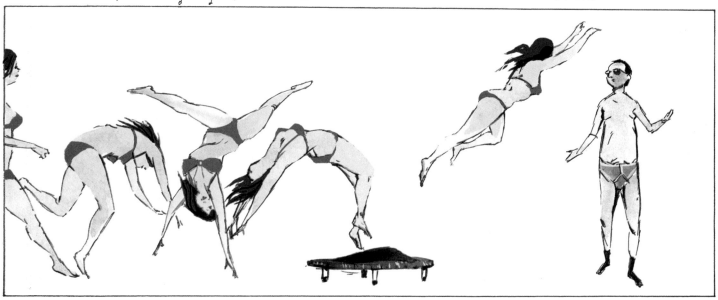

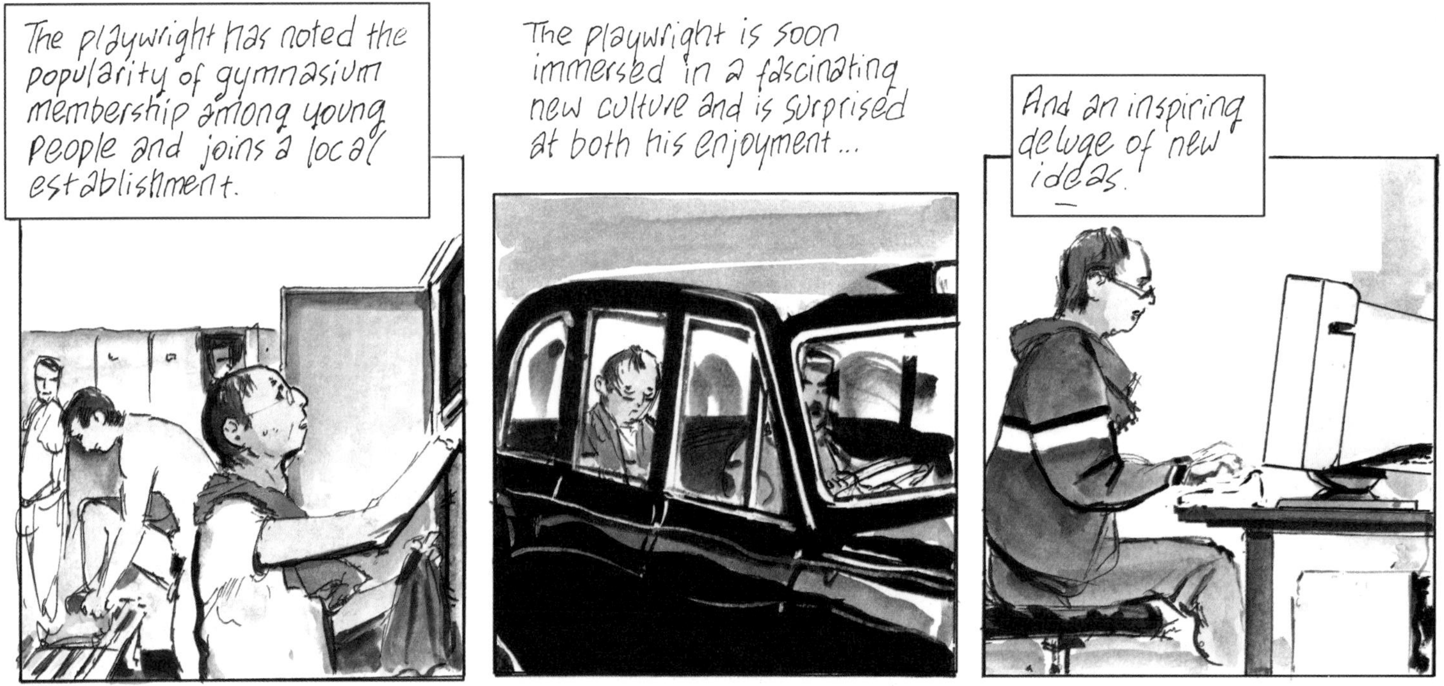

The playwright has noted the popularity of gymnasium membership among young people and joins a local establishment.
The playwright is soon immersed in a fascinating new culture and is surprised at both his enjoyment ...
And an inspiring deluge of new ideas.

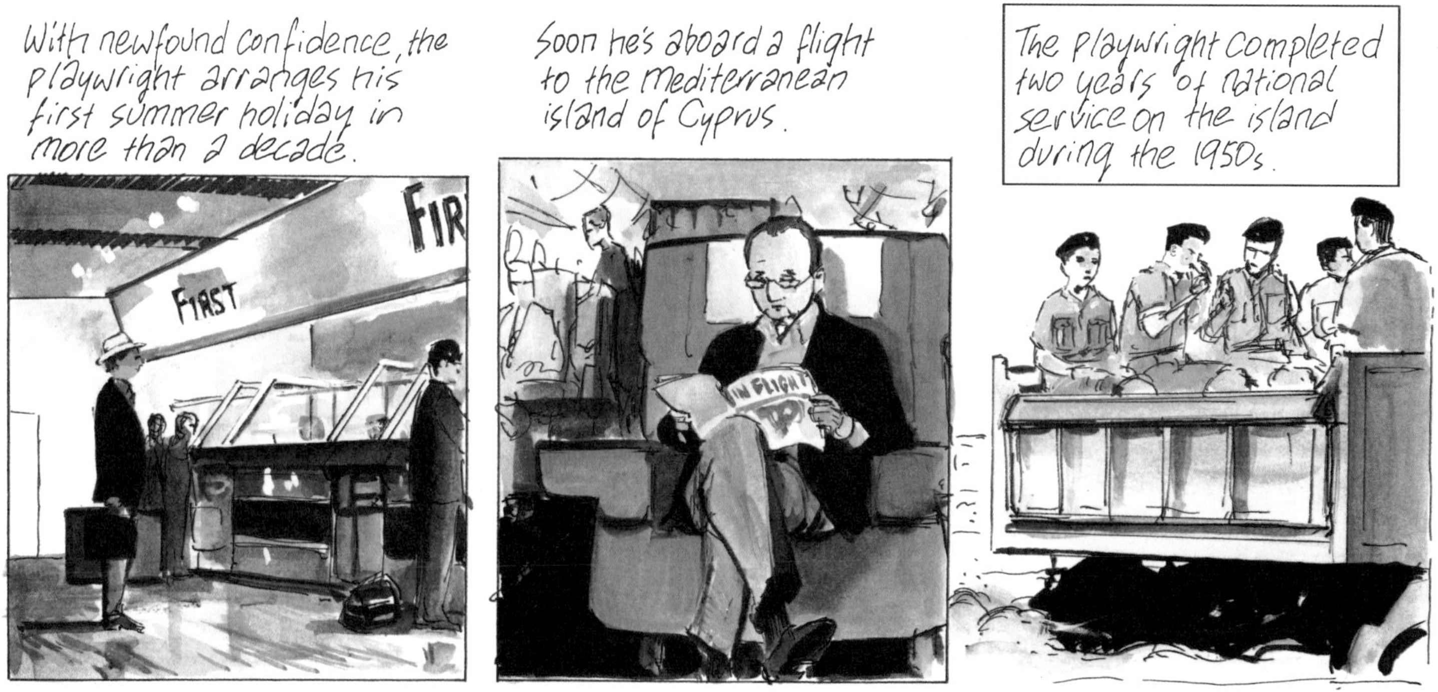
With newfound confidence, the playwright arranges his first summer holiday in more than a decade.
FIR
FIRST
Soon he's aboard a flight to the Mediterranean island of Cyprus.
IN FLIGHT
The playwright completed two years of national service on the island during the 1950s.

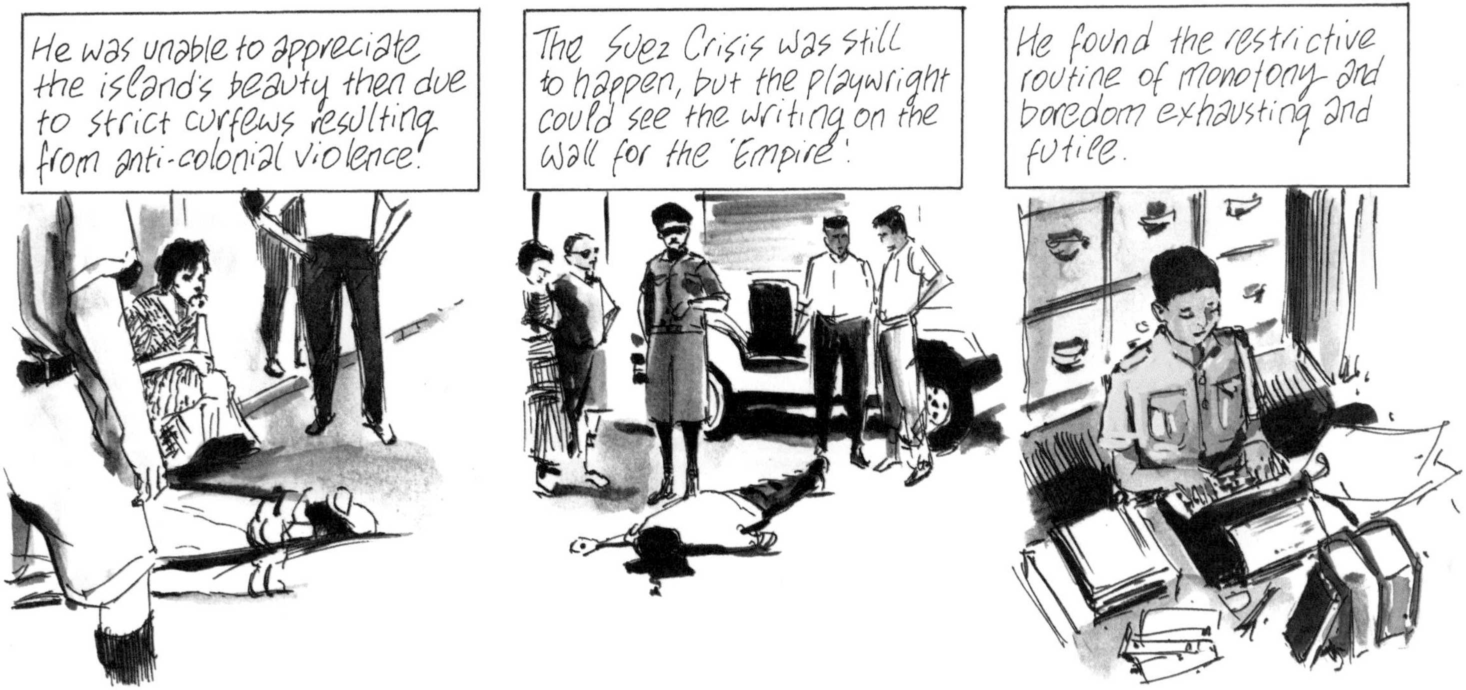
He was unable to appreciate the island's beauty then due to strict curfews resulting from anti-colonial violence.
The Suez Crisis was still to happen, but the playwright could see the writing on the wall for the 'Empire'.
He found the restrictive routine of monotony and boredom exhausting and futile.

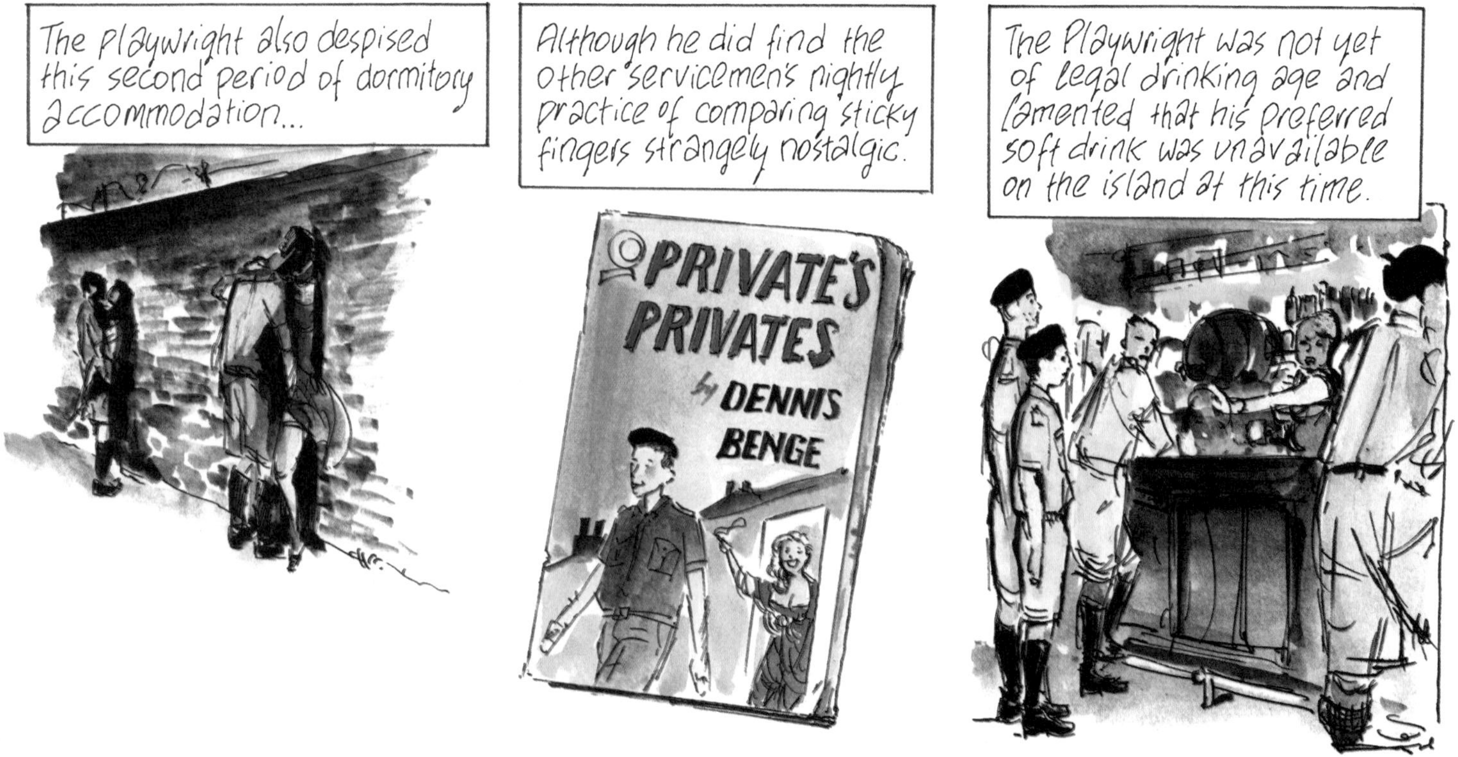
The playwright also despised this second period of dormitory accommodation...
Although he did find the other servicemen's nightly practice of comparing sticky fingers strangely nostalgic.
PRIVATE'S PRIVATES
by DENNIS BENGE
The Playwright was not yet of legal drinking age and lamented that his preferred soft drink was unavailable on the island at this time.

With customary diligence, he soon established himself as the beverage importation agent and within six months was supplying branded soft drink to the whole of Cyprus.

By the time he completed his second year, he had generated sufficient funds to finance a full-time writing career.

In fact, from the time he was discharged and returned to Britain, the playwright was never directly employed again.

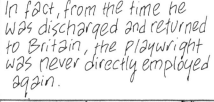

Halfway through the second week of his holiday, the playwright falls into conversation with a wealthy lady similarly aged to himself.

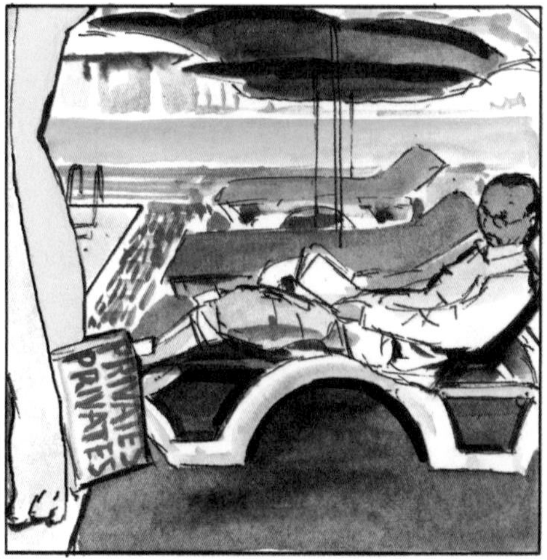
PRIVATES
PRIVATES

The lady is quite knowledgeable about his work and seems genuinely interested in a number of his personal anecdotes.

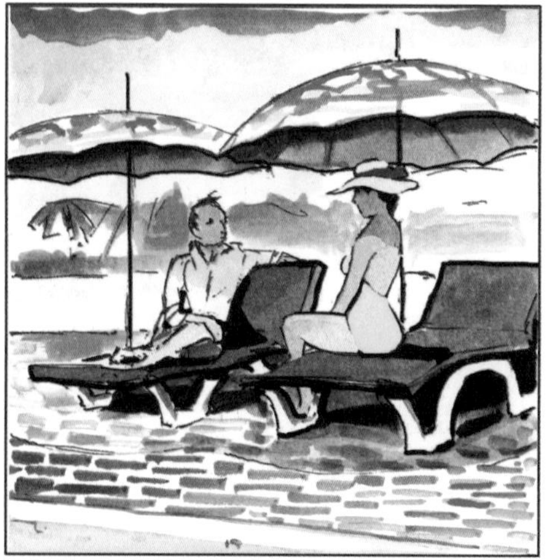

The playwright's low personal confidence usually renders him too embarrassed to interact with female fans of his work.

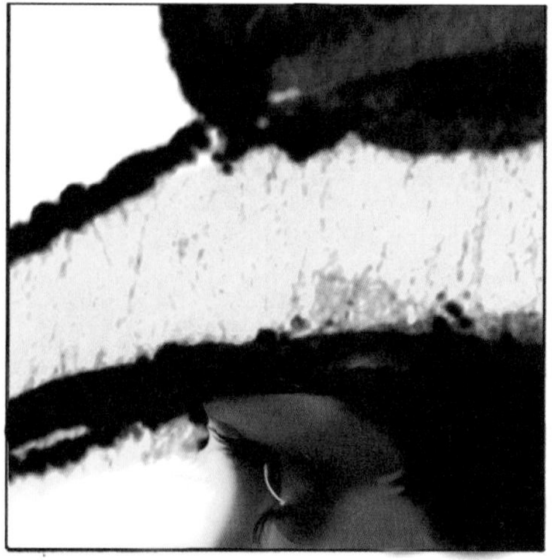

However, the lady's enthusiasm places him at ease and his conversation sparkles in a manner that usually evades him.

The couple dines together for three consecutive nights and he learns that she was widowed quite early in life...

and that while continuing her husband's business and raising her daughter, has never found the time for romance.

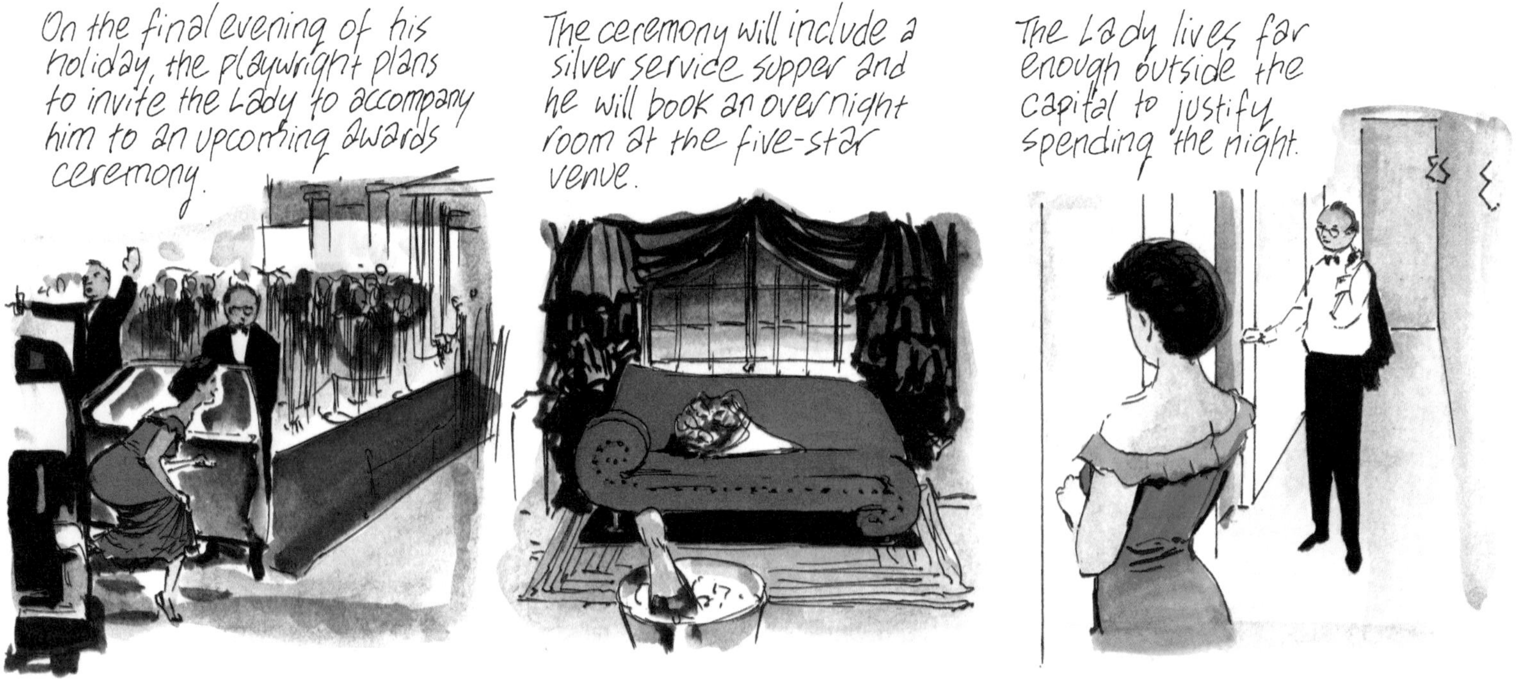
On the final evening of his holiday, the playwright plans to invite the Lady to accompany him to an upcoming awards ceremony.
The ceremony will include a silver service supper and he will book an overnight room at the five-star venue.
The Lady lives far enough outside the capital to justify spending the night.

And so he will reserve the adjoining suite to accommodate all potential outcomes.

However, as he waits for her to join him at the bar, he overhears a group of men discussing the Lady's bikini line.

He is horrified when one
of the men boasts that
she offered to perform
fellatio on him.

The playwright
never speaks
to the Lady
again.

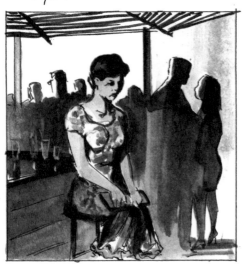

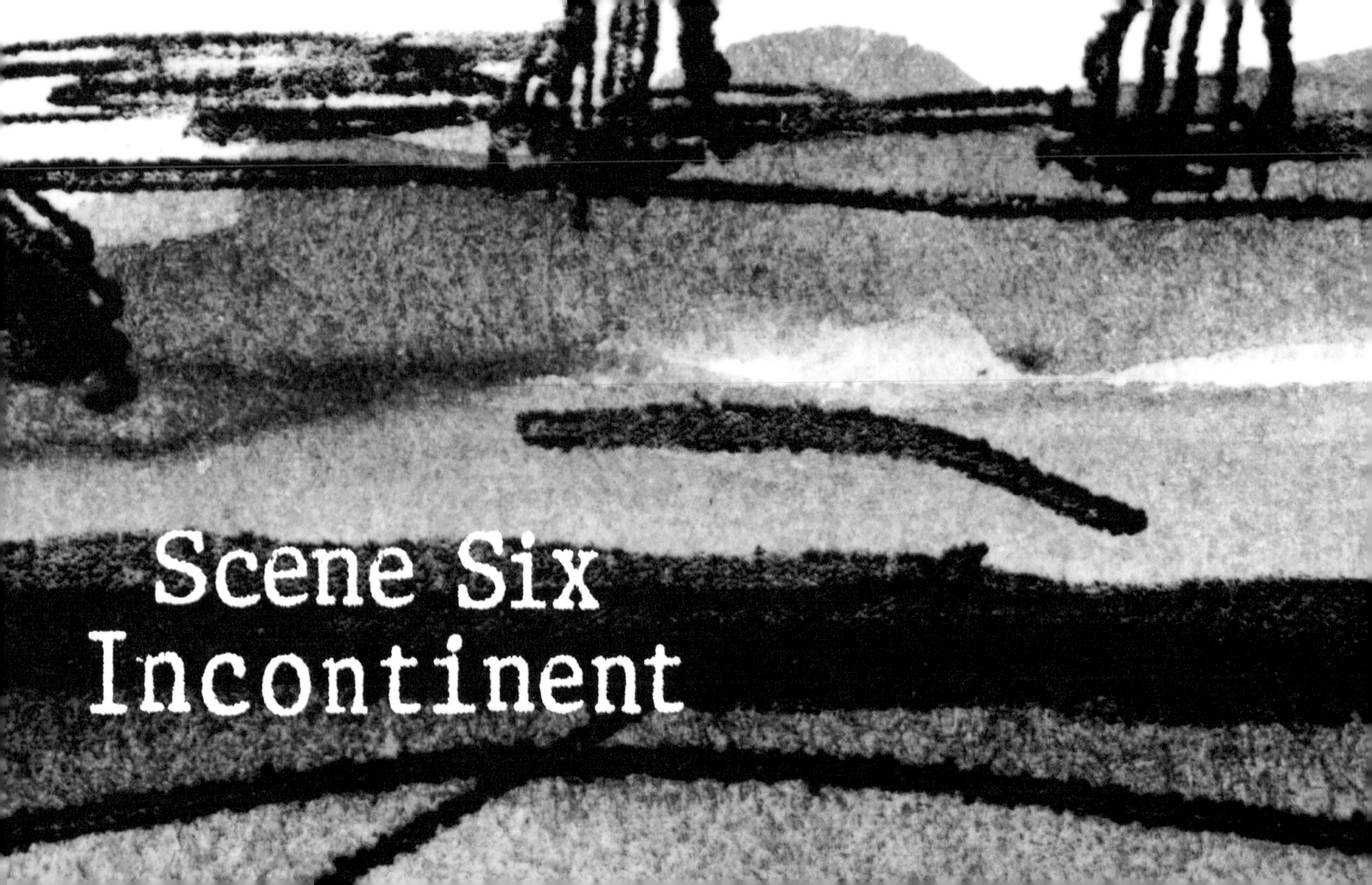

Scene Six
Incontinent

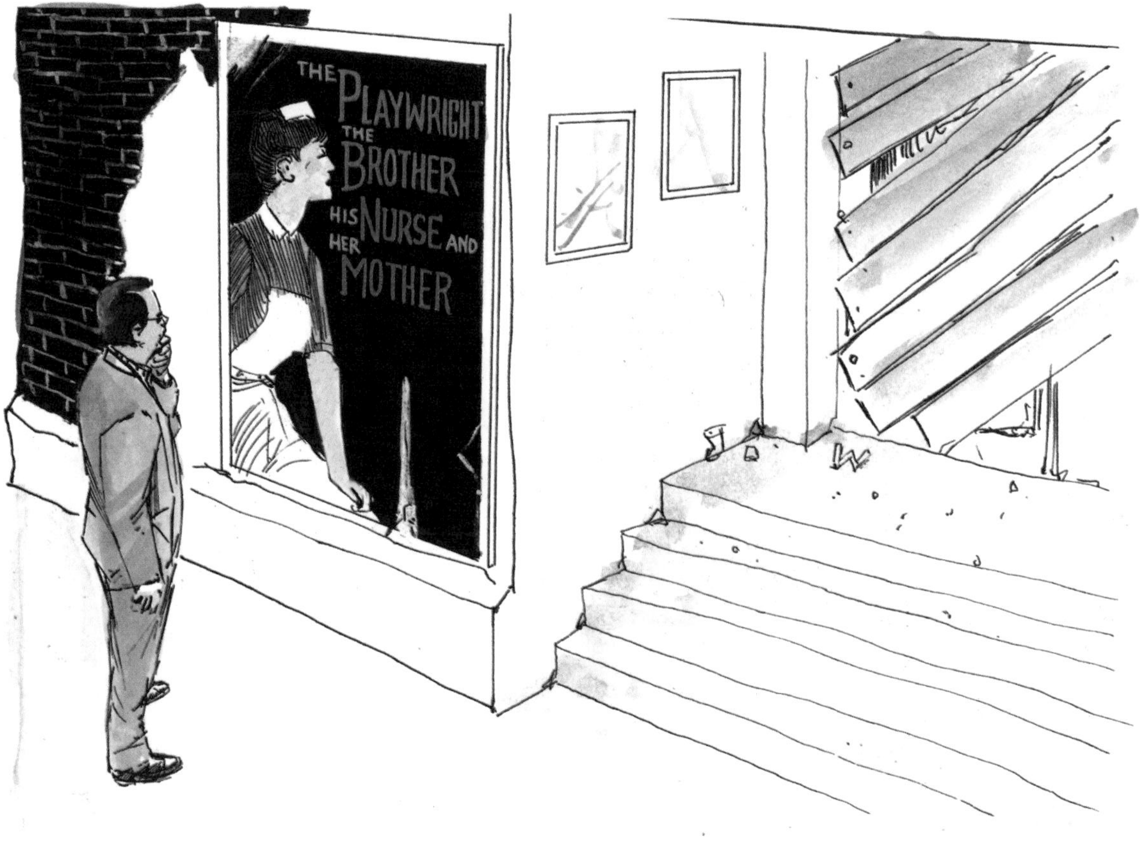
THE PLAYWRIGHT
THE BROTHER
HIS NURSE AND
HER MOTHER

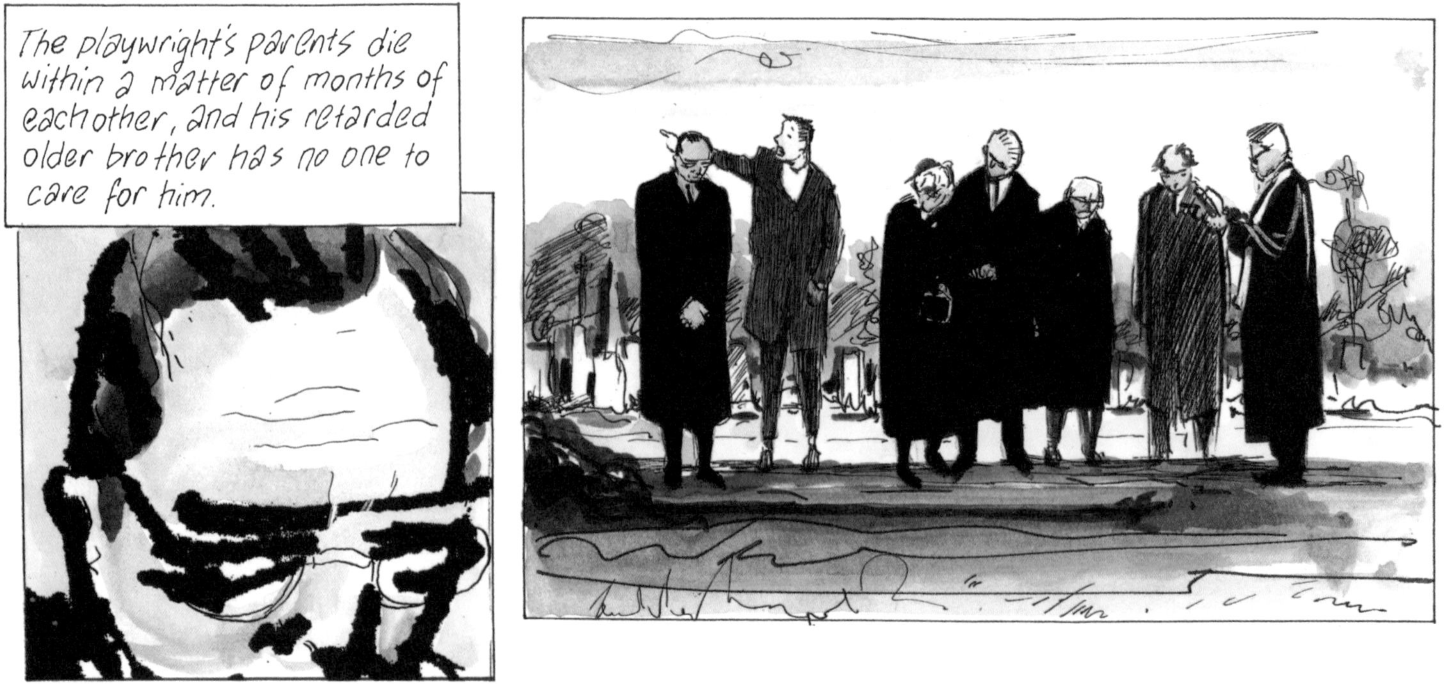
The playwright's parents die within a matter of months of eachother, and his retarded older brother has no one to care for him.

The Playwright had not made peace with his mother before she died and suffers tremendous guilt during his time of grieving.

Although financially comfortable, the playwright decides against placing his retarded older brother in a commercial nursing establishment...

...preferring instead to engage a residential nurse at his home, and convert the study into a crèche.

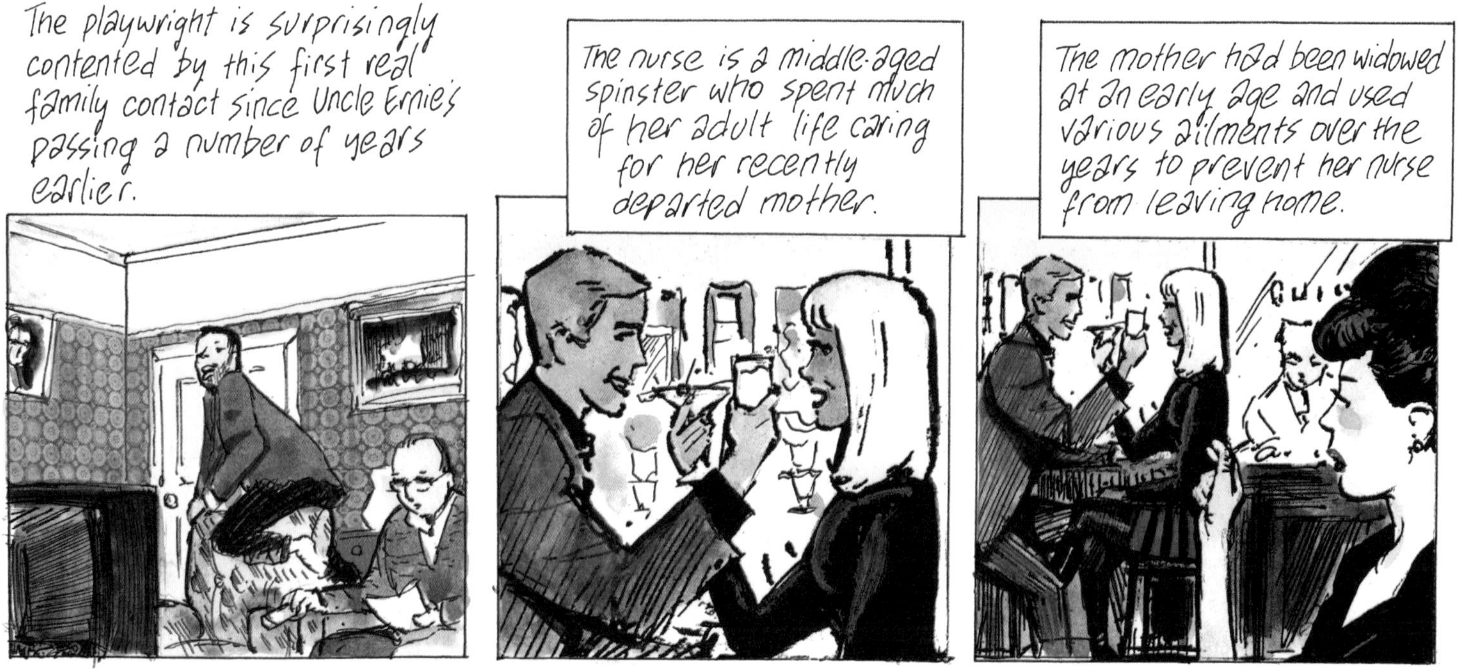
The playwright is surprisingly contented by this first real family contact since Uncle Ernie's passing a number of years earlier.
The nurse is a middle-aged spinster who spent much of her adult life caring for her recently departed mother.
The mother had been widowed at an early age and used various ailments over the years to prevent her nurse from leaving home.

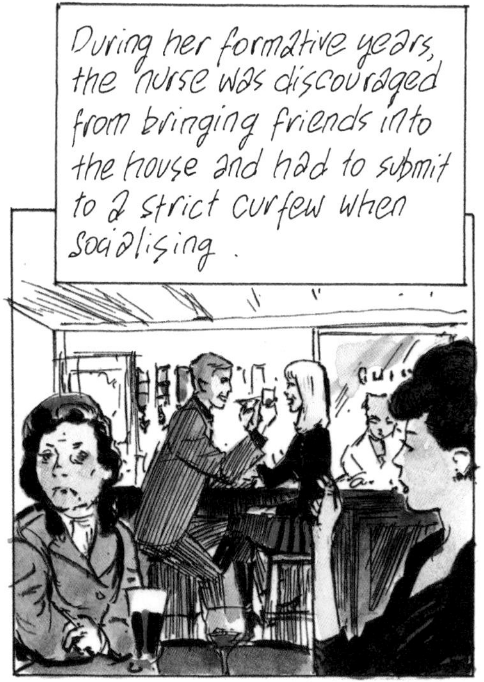
During her formative years, the nurse was discouraged from bringing friends into the house and had to submit to a strict curfew when socialising.

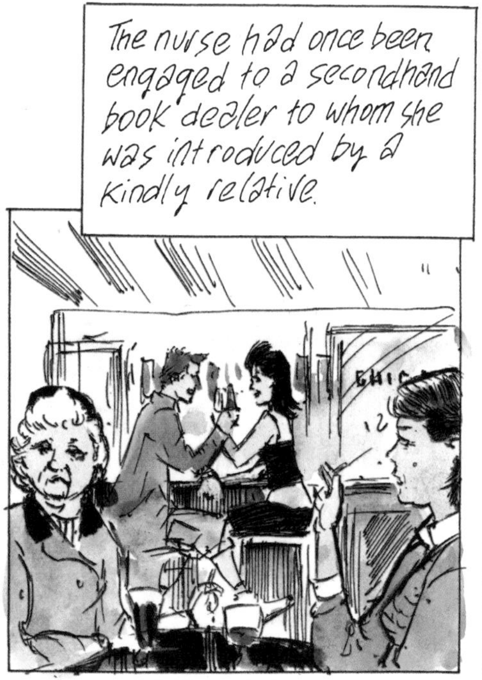
The nurse had once been engaged to a secondhand book dealer to whom she was introduced by a kindly relative.

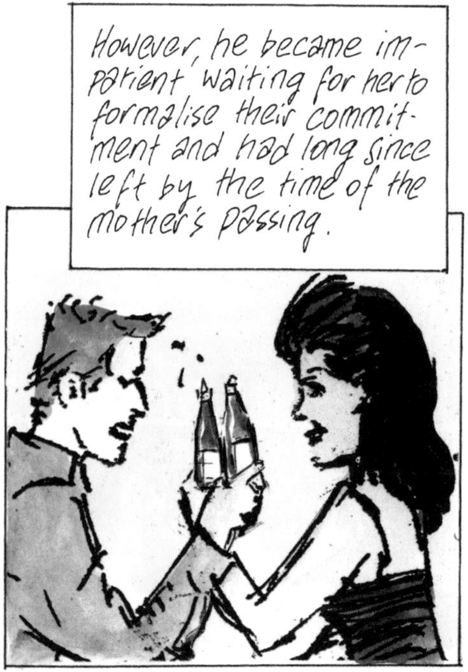
However, he became impatient waiting for her to formalise their commitment and had long since left by the time of the mother's passing.

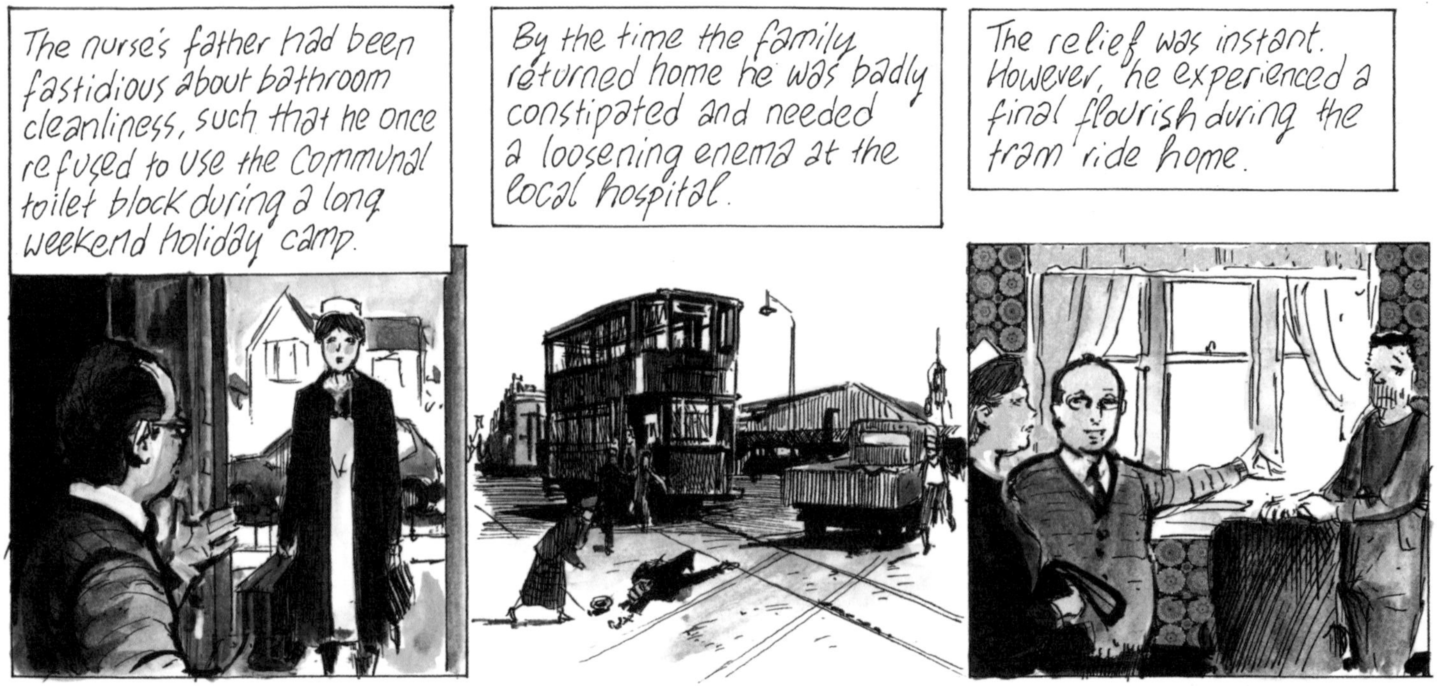
The nurse's father had been fastidious about bathroom cleanliness, such that he once refused to use the communal toilet block during a long weekend holiday camp.
By the time the family returned home he was badly constipated and needed a loosening enema at the local hospital.
The relief was instant. However, he experienced a final flourish during the tram ride home.

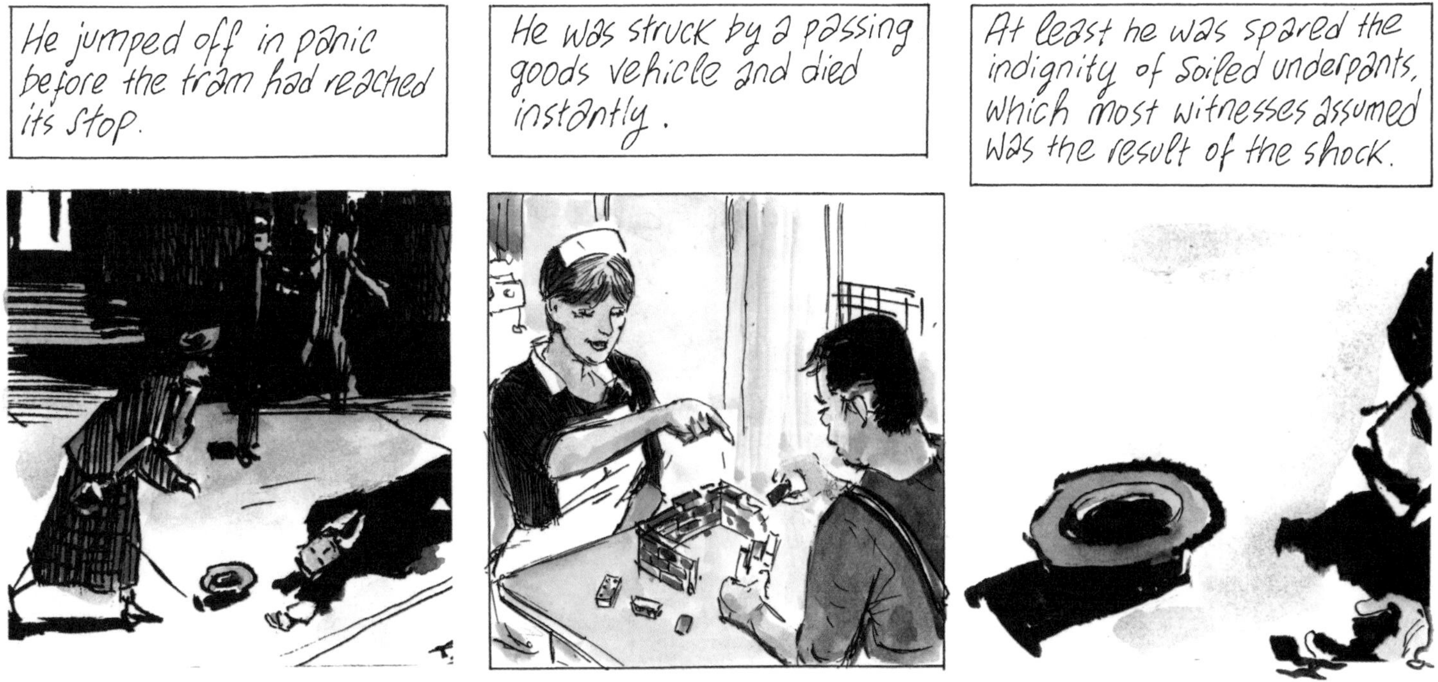
He jumped off in panic before the tram had reached its stop.
He was struck by a passing goods vehicle and died instantly.
At least he was spared the indignity of soiled underpants, which most witnesses assumed was the result of the shock.

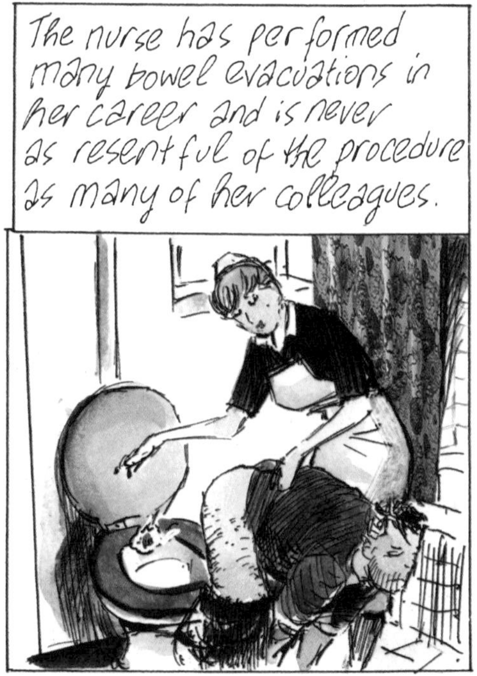
The nurse has performed many bowel evacuations in her career and is never as resentful of the procedure as many of her colleagues.
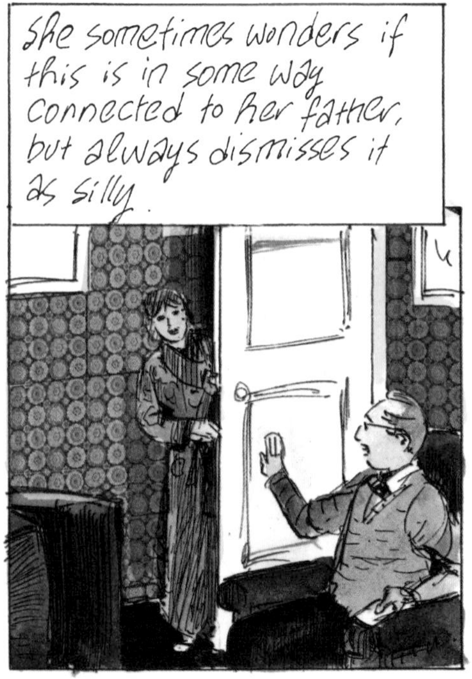
She sometimes wonders if this is in some way connected to her father, but always dismisses it as silly.
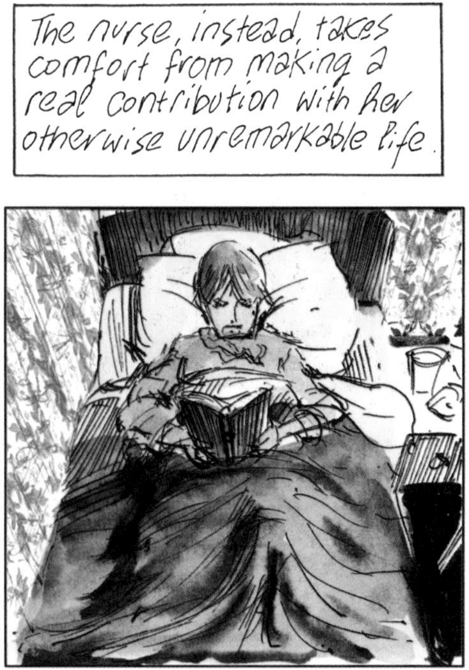
The nurse, instead, takes comfort from making a real contribution with her otherwise unremarkable life.

The playwright conscientiously subscribes to a number of women's magazines to keep in touch with contemporary issues facing the modern girl...

..and is somewhat intrigued to learn that the 21 to 30 decile prefer their partners circumcised.

The playwright wants to appear a considerate lover and, for a while, considers a voluntary medical procedure.

However, he is intimidated by the notion that the nursing staff might judge his anaesthetized penis...

...and resolves instead to pay particular attention to genital cleanliness during his morning bath.

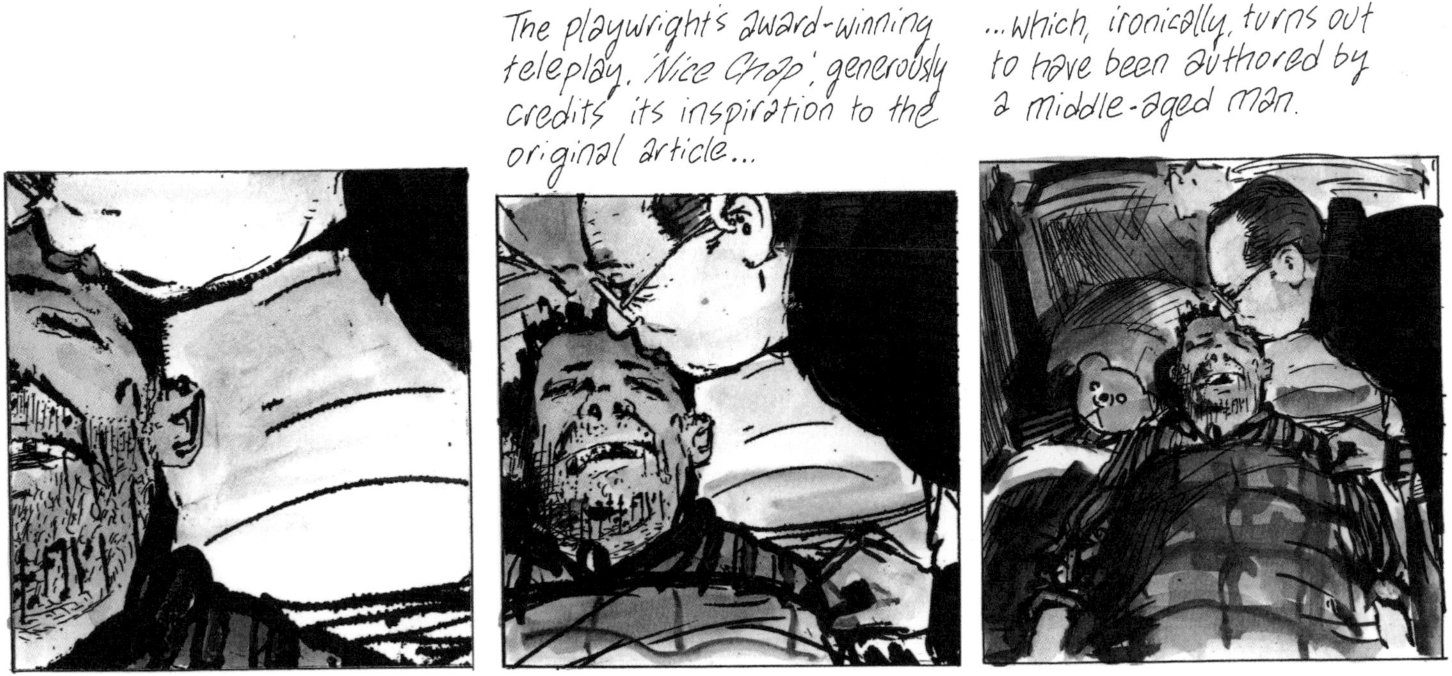
The playwright's award-winning teleplay, 'Nice Chap', generously credits its inspiration to the original article...
...which, ironically, turns out to have been authored by a middle-aged man.

The playwright's retarded older brother is incontinent and also fond of rubbing himself against various objects around the house.

His movie treatment, '*Gripping Hands and Realistic Hair,*' was largely inspired by the brother's collection of vintage action-man dolls.

The brother has an uncanny knack of defecating during meal times and the playwright feels sympathetic to young families with untrained infants.

He is embarrassed that the nurse has to experience such occurrences and tremendously admires her silent fortitude when addressing the clean-up.

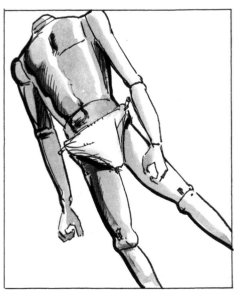

Scene Seven
Appendix

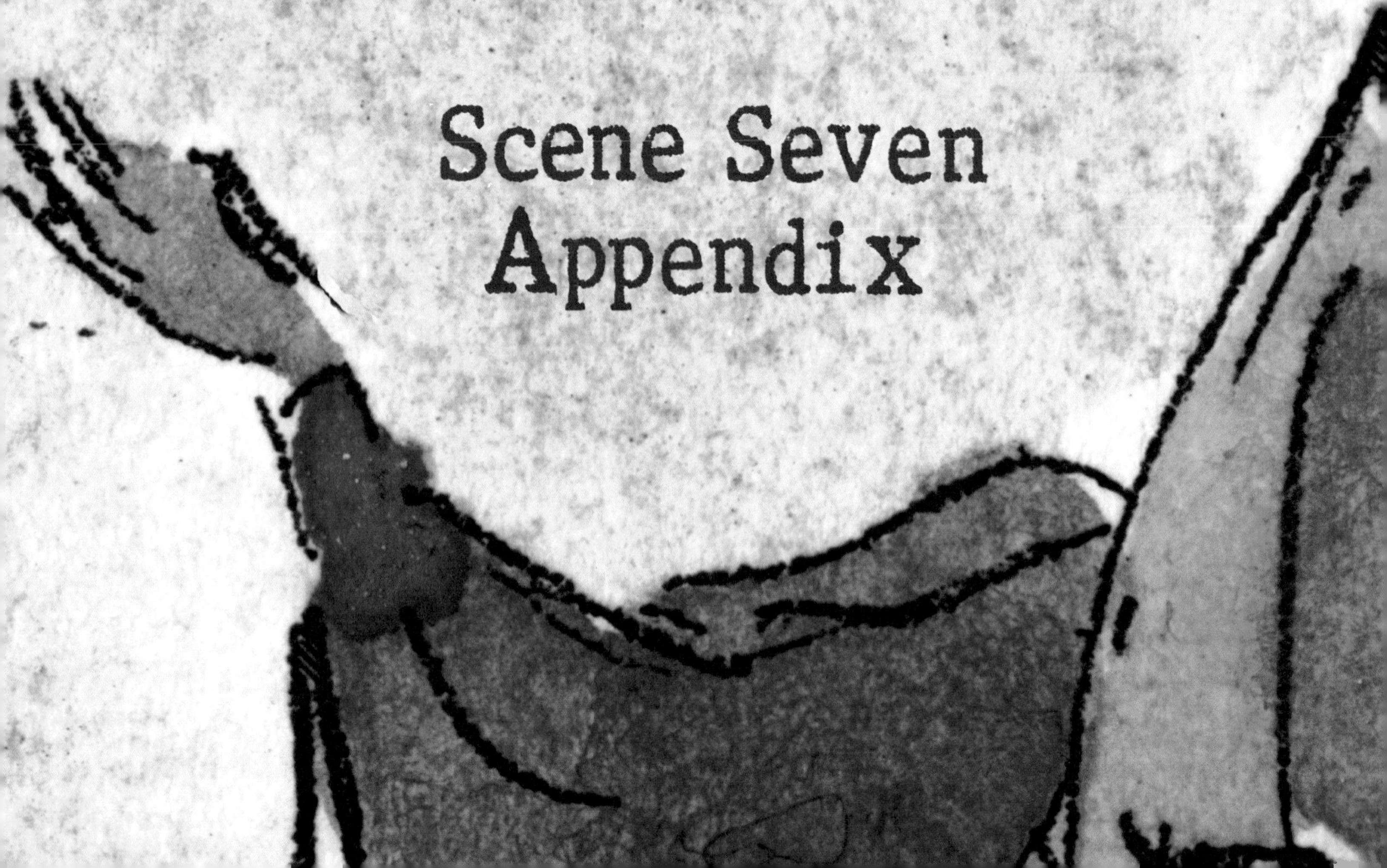

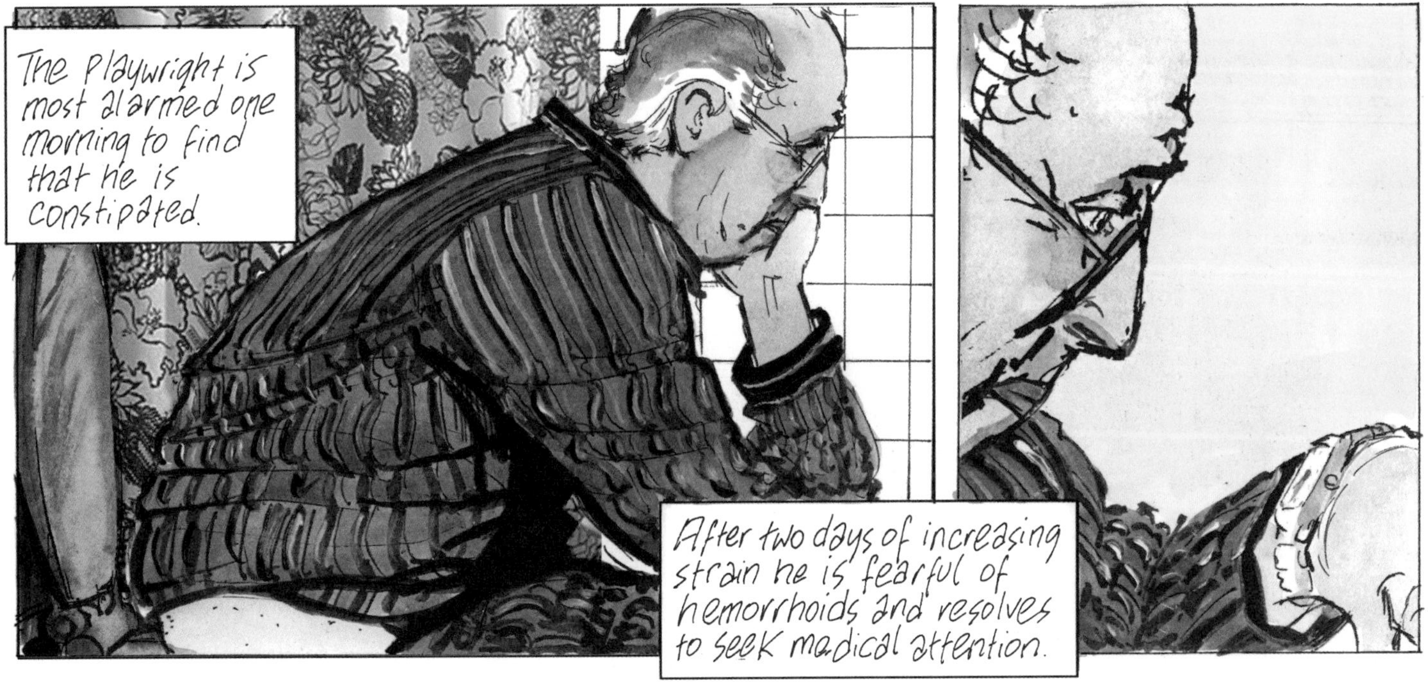
The playwright is most alarmed one morning to find that he is constipated.
After two days of increasing strain he is fearful of hemorrhoids and resolves to seek medical attention.

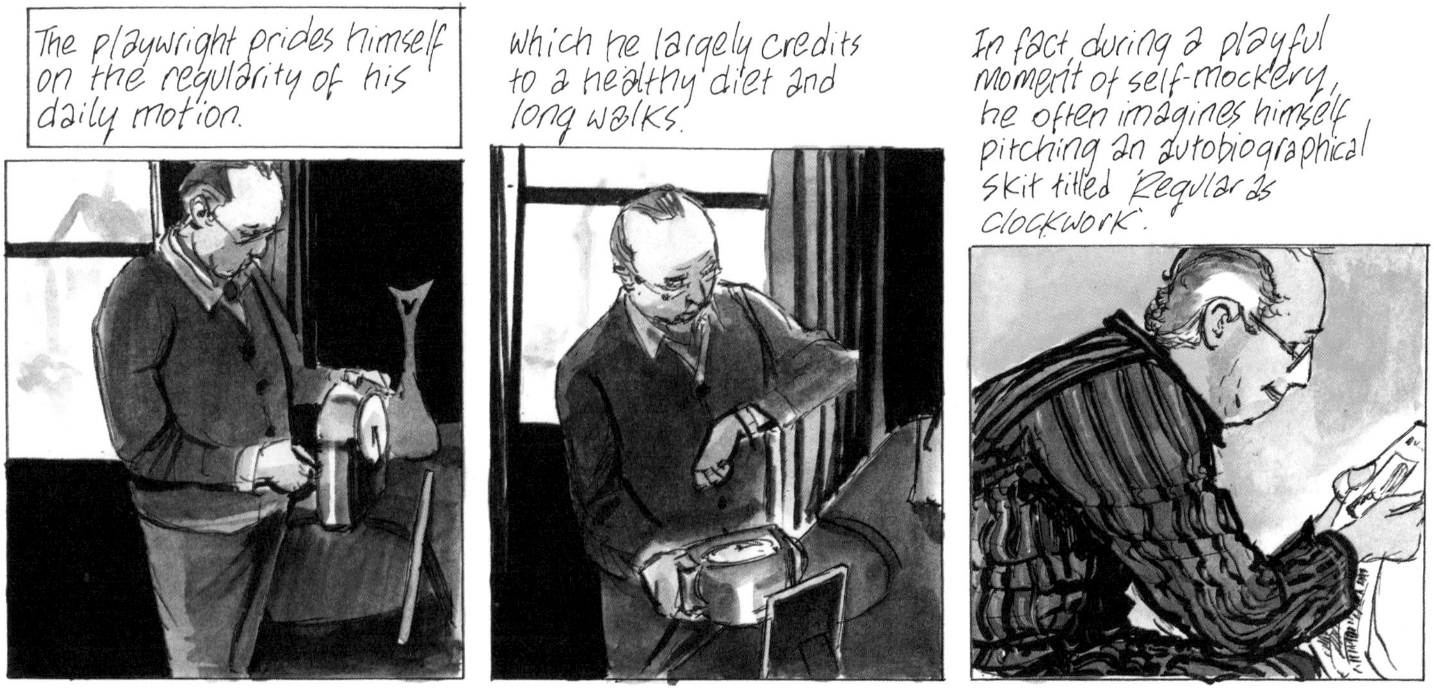
The playwright prides himself on the regularity of his daily motion.
which he largely credits to a healthy diet and long walks.
In fact, during a playful moment of self-mockery, he often imagines himself pitching an autobiographical skit titled 'Regular as clockwork'.

The playwright's usual doctor is away on annual leave and his locum is a rather attractive lady in her late thirties.

The playwright is rendered speechless when she requests that he drop his trousers...

to allow her to perform a rectal examination.

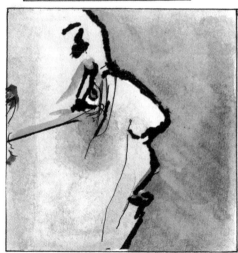

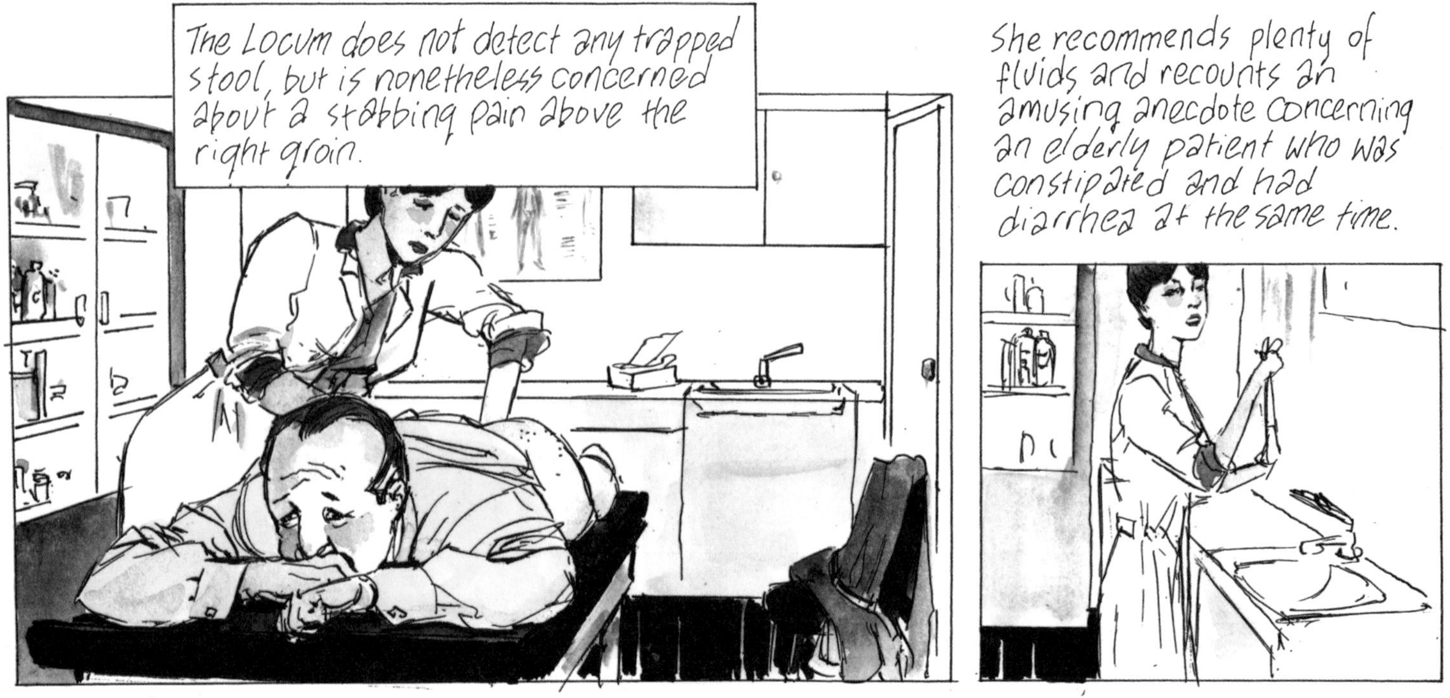
The Locum does not detect any trapped stool, but is nonetheless concerned about a stabbing pain above the right groin.
She recommends plenty of fluids and recounts an amusing anecdote concerning an elderly patient who was constipated and had diarrhea at the same time.

The playwright is relieved when his usual constitution resumes that evening.

And he marks the occasion with a nice glass of aged Semillon.

He is later awoken in the middle of the night by excruciating pain and collapses on the way to the bathroom.

Fortunately his brother's nurse hears his crying and, suspecting appendicitis, immediately calls an ambulance.

Within the hour the playwright lies medicated in a preoperative suite while an Australian male nurse,

ironically born near the vineyard that made the nice Semillon, shaves his pubic hair.

The Nurse correctly surmises that the playwrights appendix is perforated and an emergency operation is performed.

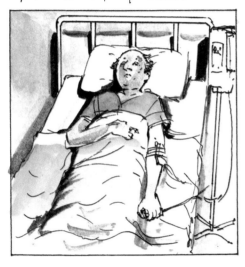

He spends three nights in hospital and bizarrely feels almost special...

When the doctor explains that the complaint is quite rare in a man of his age.

A self-administering morphine
drip is connected during
the first twenty-four hours.

And the Playwright is
elated at the ease with
which he can blank his mind.

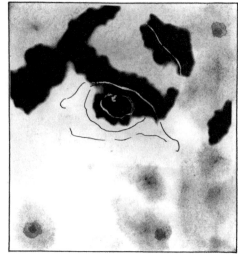

However, he fears that the
wall-mounted television is
plotting to steal his next script.

He is secretly relieved the
following day when a nurse
informs him that oral
pain relief will now suffice.

Immediately prior to his dis-
charge, the playwright gathers
notes for a stream-of-
consciousness approach...

to the 'memoirs of a slave
Princess' genre, tentatively
titled 'They stitched me up.'

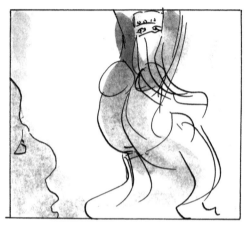

clarity resumes and he
quickly abandons the
idea as foolhardy.

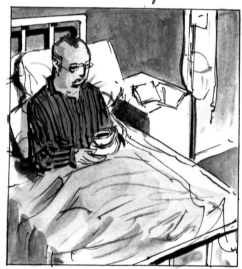

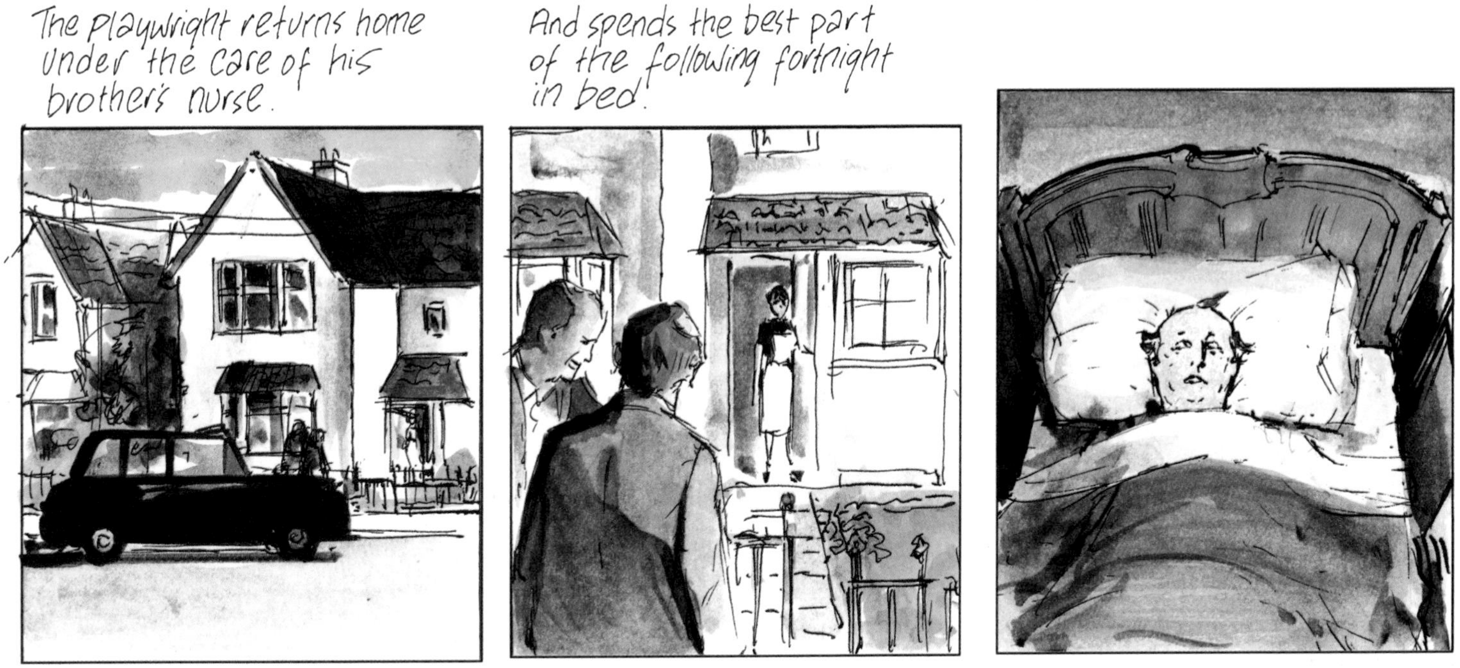
The playwright returns home under the care of his brother's nurse.
And spends the best part of the following fortnight in bed.

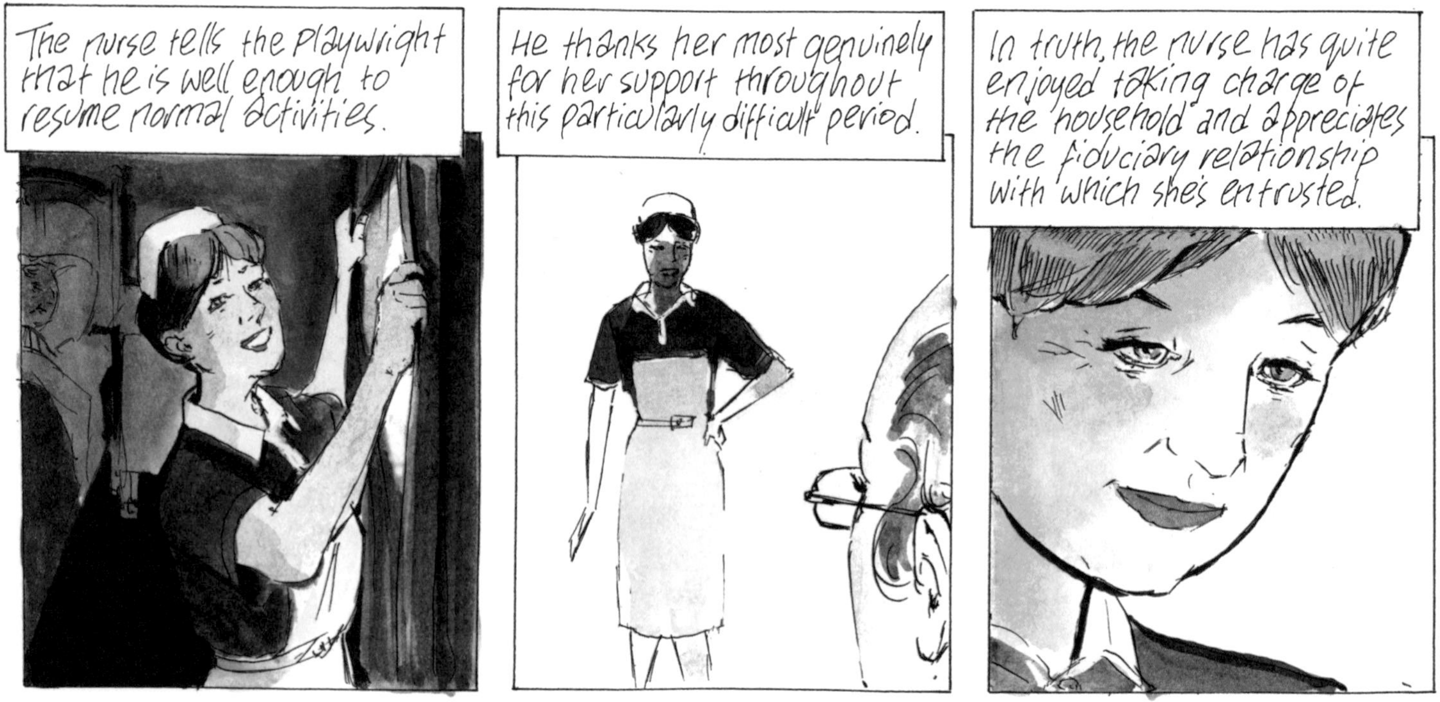
The nurse tells the playwright that he is well enough to resume normal activities.
He thanks her most genuinely for her support throughout this particularly difficult period.
In truth, the nurse has quite enjoyed taking charge of the household and appreciates the fiduciary relationship with which she's entrusted.

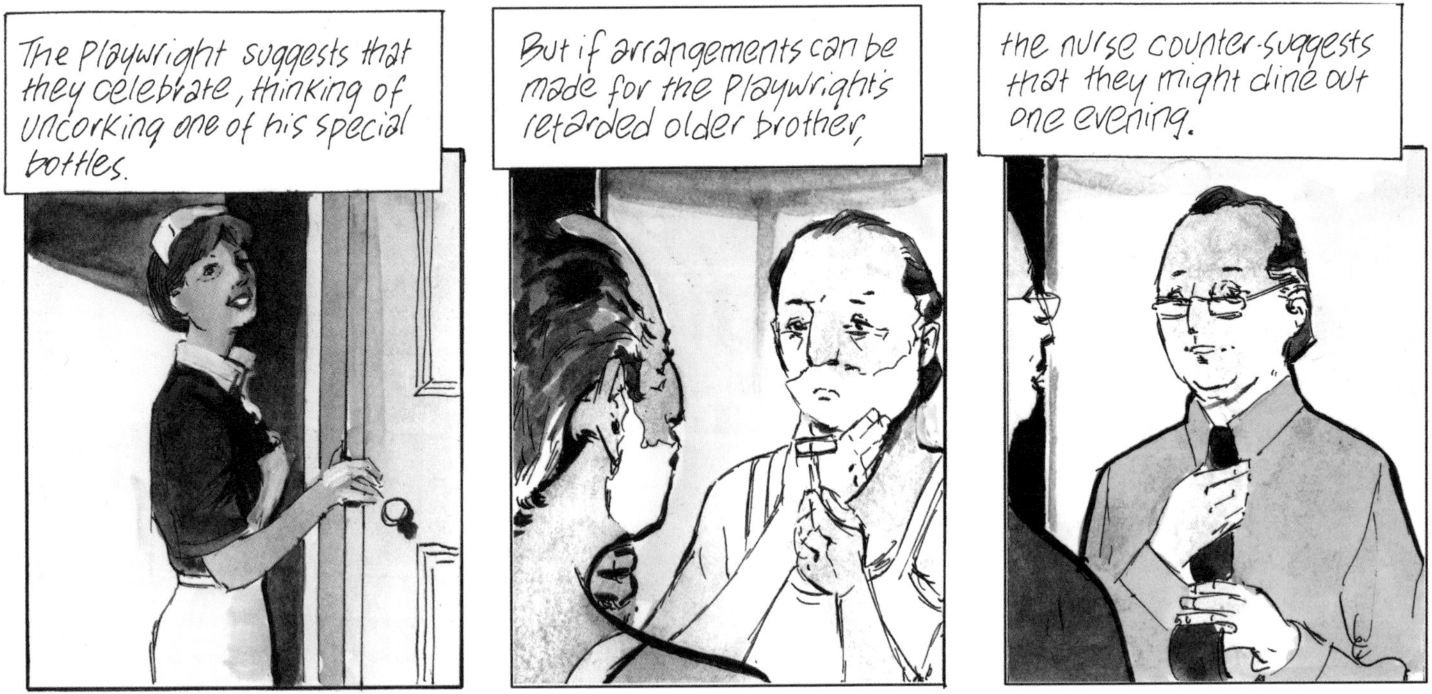
The Playwright suggests that they celebrate, thinking of uncorking one of his special bottles.
But if arrangements can be made for the Playwright's retarded older brother,
the nurse counter-suggests that they might dine out one evening.

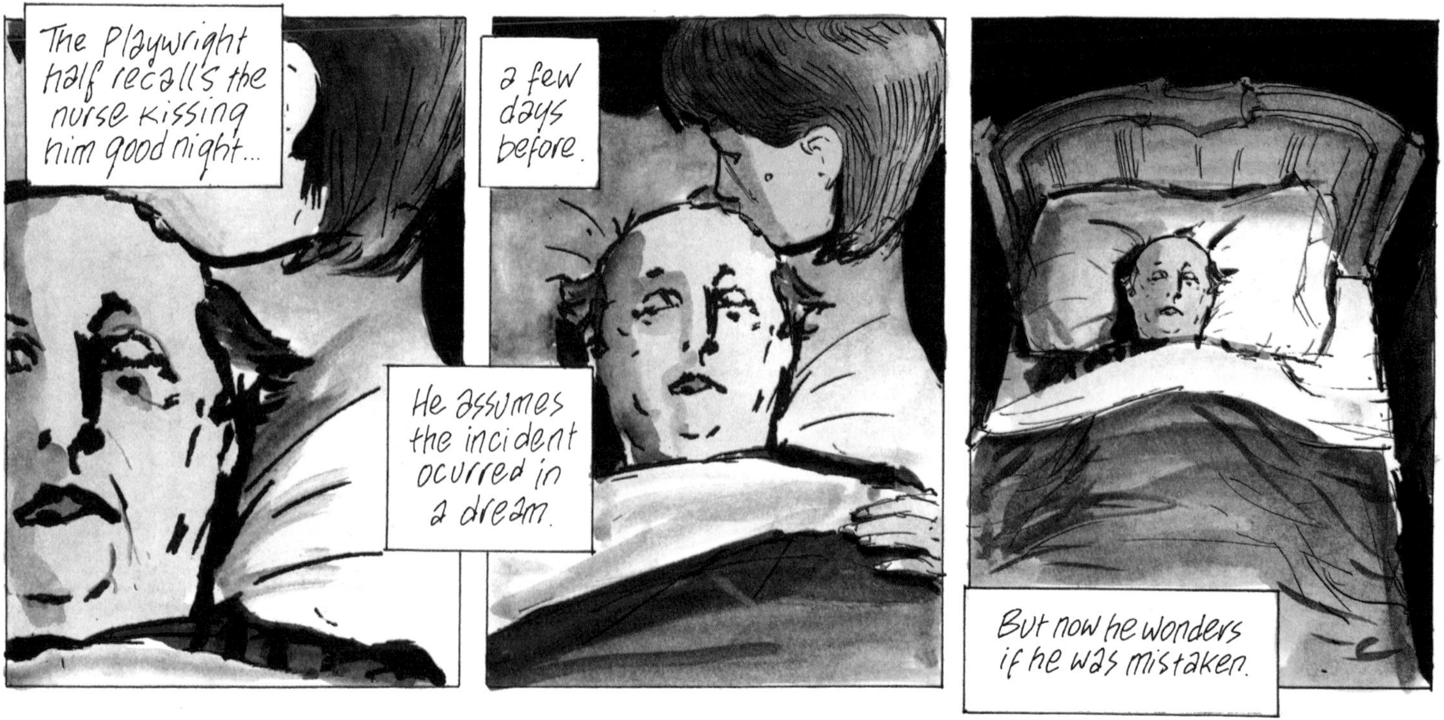
The playwright half recalls the nurse kissing him good night...
a few days before.
He assumes the incident ocurred in a dream.
But now he wonders if he was mistaken.

A few weeks later the nurse accompanies the playwright to his favourite restaurant.

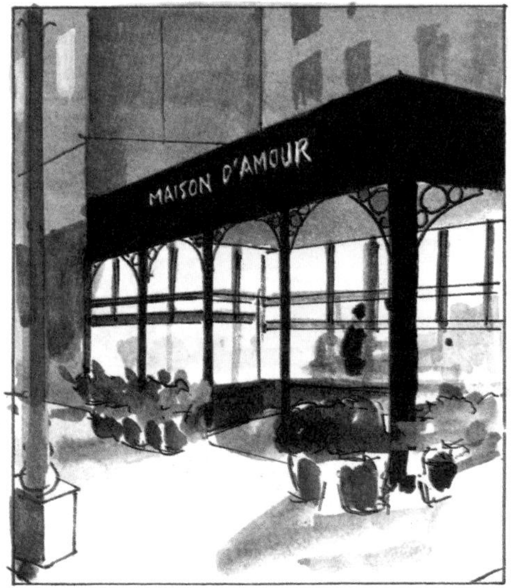
MAISON D'AMOUR

As they are directed to his usual table, he feels a vice-like grip of anxiety.

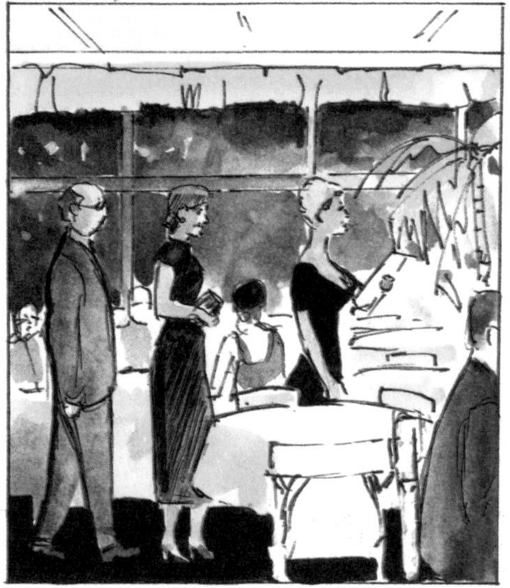

Which worsens once he realizes that his favourite waitress will be attending to their table.

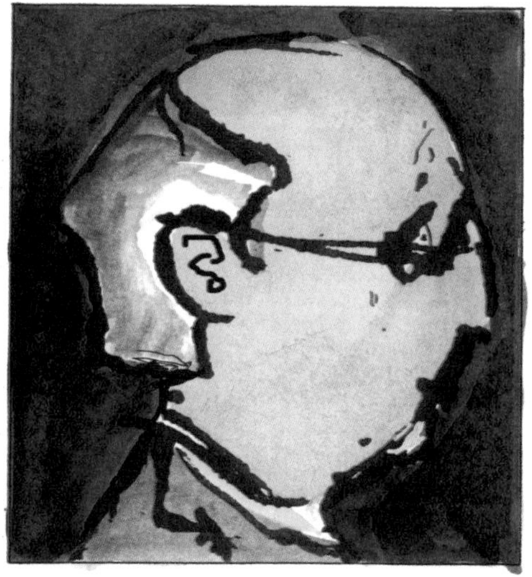

As the evening progresses, the playwright is surprised to find himself increasingly relaxed.

And his generous tip at the end of the meal is a good indication of how much he has enjoyed the experience.

The nurse thanks him with a kiss on the cheek.

The Playwright reflects that he has not once had to abruptly avert his stare from the waitress' chest during the entire evening.

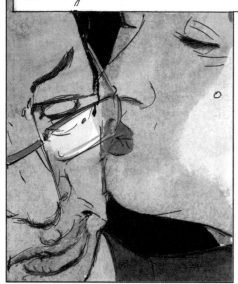
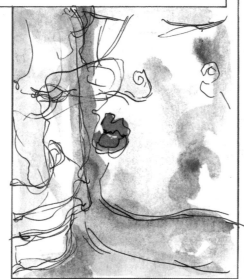

Scene Eight
An accounting

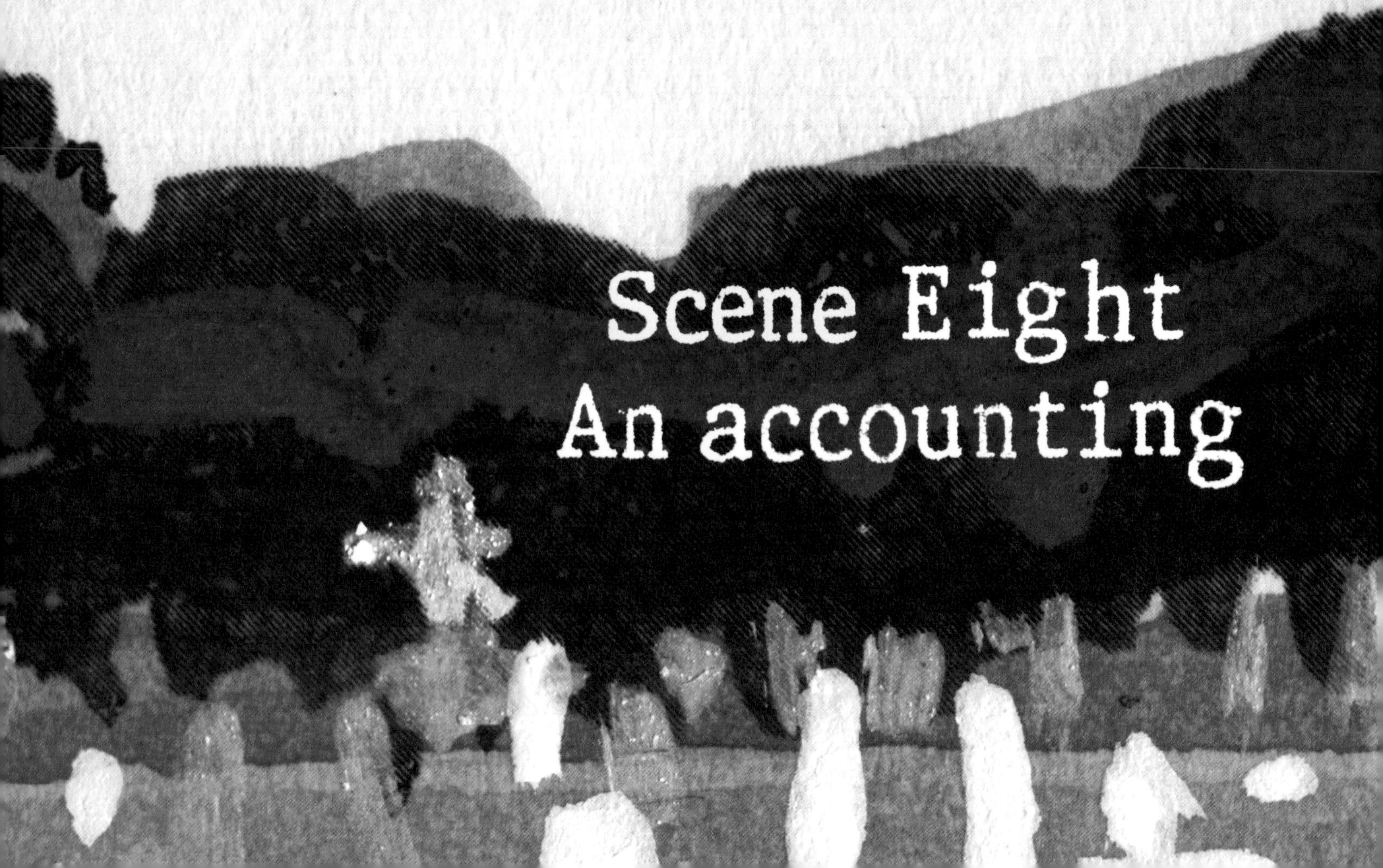

The playwright's brother dies quite suddenly.

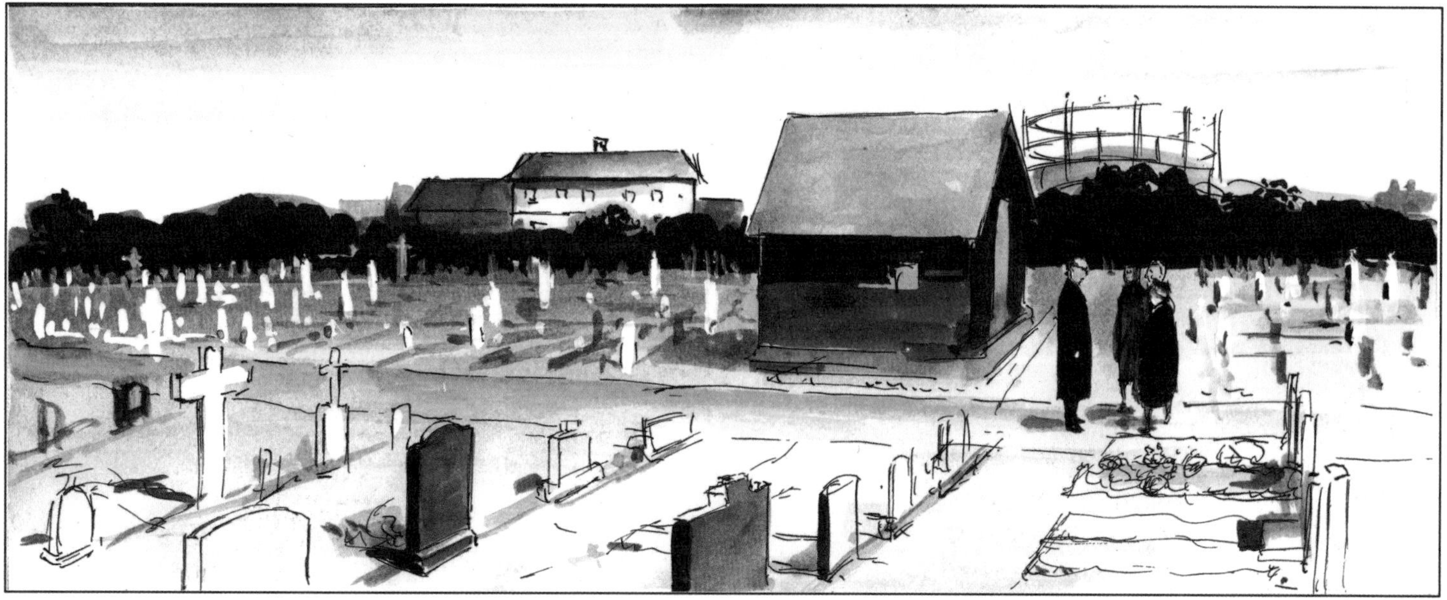

A chest infection led to pneumonia.

And within weeks it is over.

The nurse notifies a few distant cousins and attends to the funeral details with customary diligence.

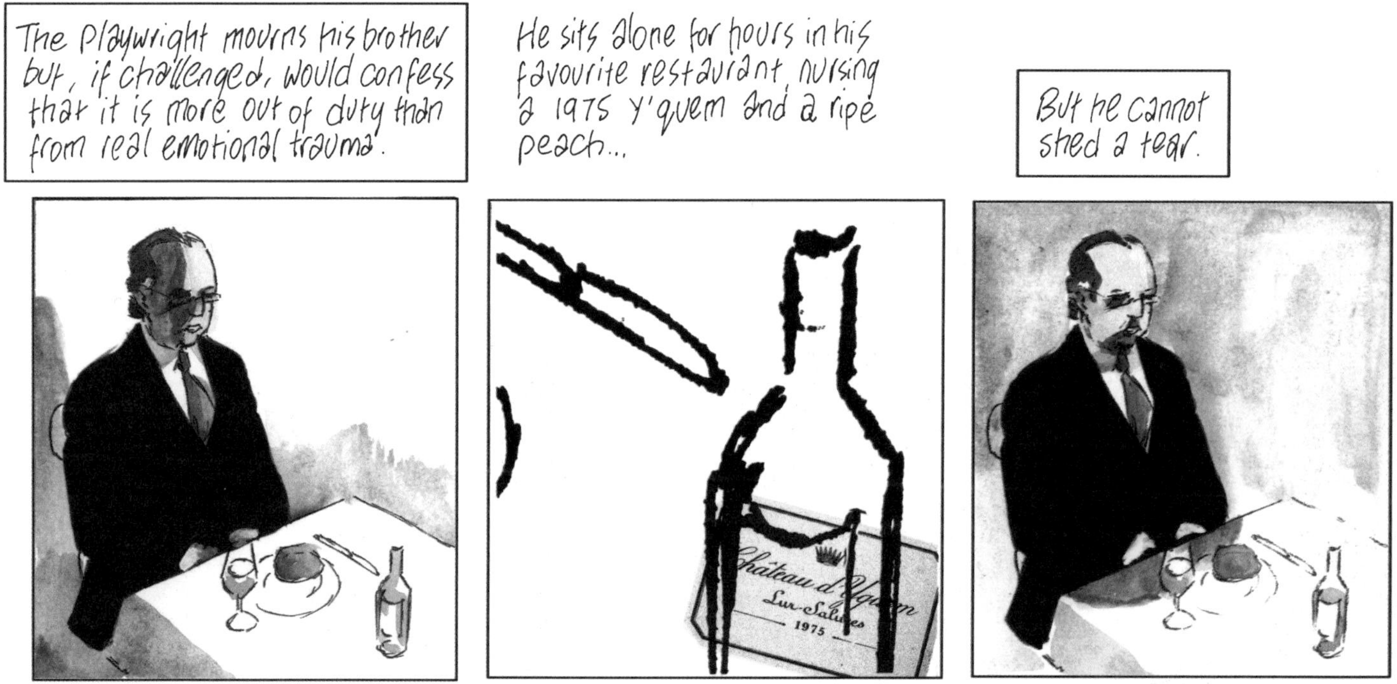
The playwright mourns his brother but, if challenged, would confess that it is more out of duty than from real emotional trauma.
He sits alone for hours in his favourite restaurant, nursing a 1975 Y'quem and a ripe peach...
1975
But he cannot shed a tear.

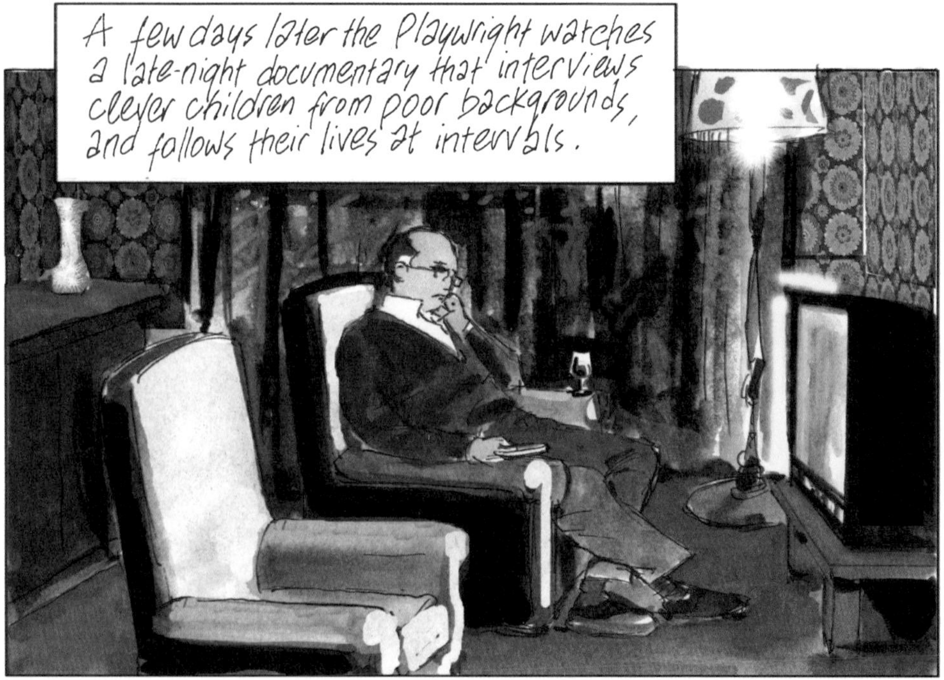
A few days later the Playwright watches a late-night documentary that interviews clever children from poor backgrounds, and follows their lives at intervals.

He is intrigued by the subject, hoping to glimpse a familiarity with his own upbringing.

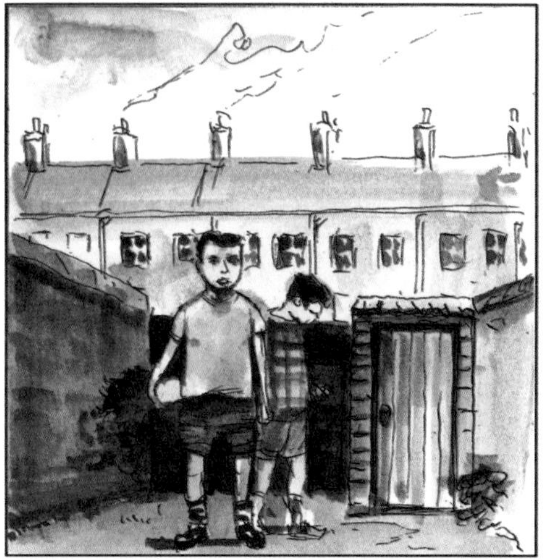

However, he is stung by the commentary of an East-end market trader who excelled in school before dropping out.

The lad reflects upon his lack of interest, discipline, and fiscal ambition, then concludes that while he considers himself happy, he covets disposable wealth.

He qualifies this so far as to say that he isn't so much jealous of his former peers' financial success as he resents their lack of creativity in enjoying it.

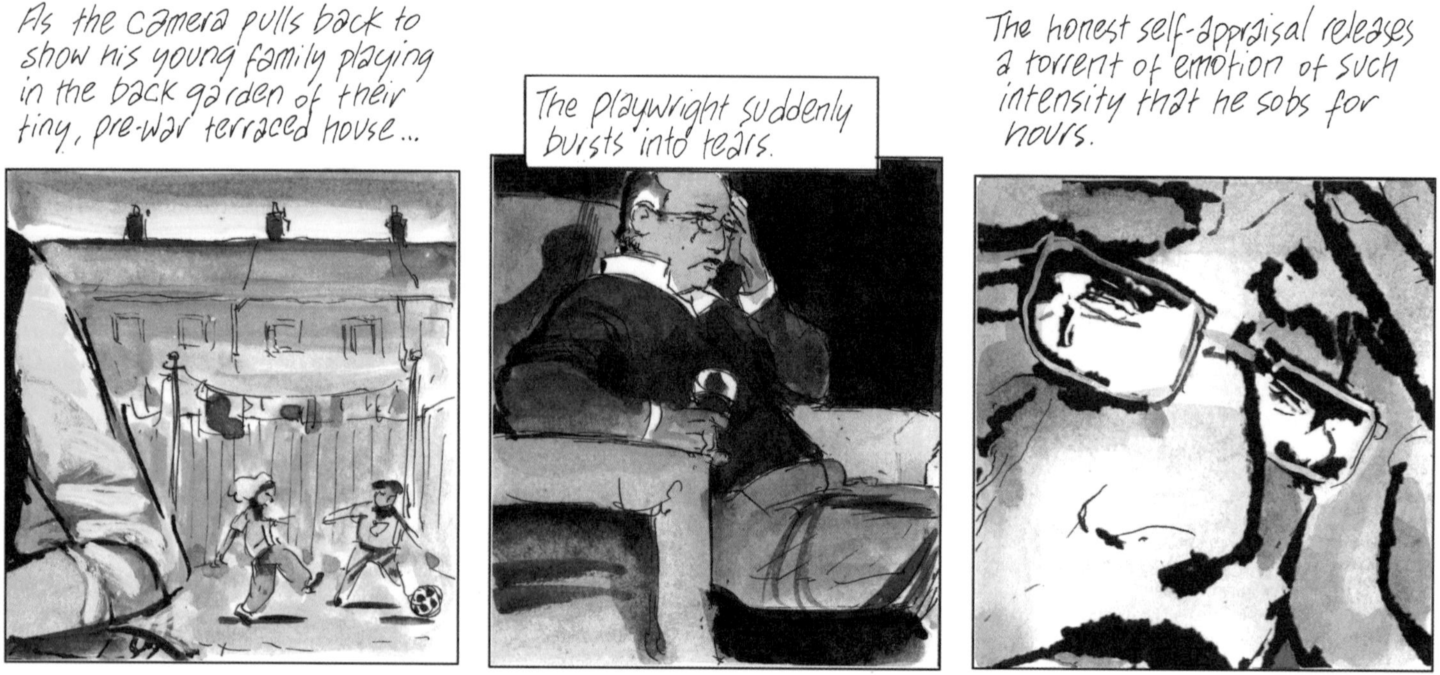
As the camera pulls back to show his young family playing in the back garden of their tiny, pre-war terraced house...
The playwright suddenly bursts into tears.
The honest self-appraisal releases a torrent of emotion of such intensity that he sobs for hours.

The playwright doesn't write another word for over three weeks, which is very unusual.

While many of his ideas are quickly discarded, he normally spends a few hours every day recording his thoughts.

He wonders whether he is depressed, but is in fact quite contented around the house and enjoys the break from his relentless mental narration.

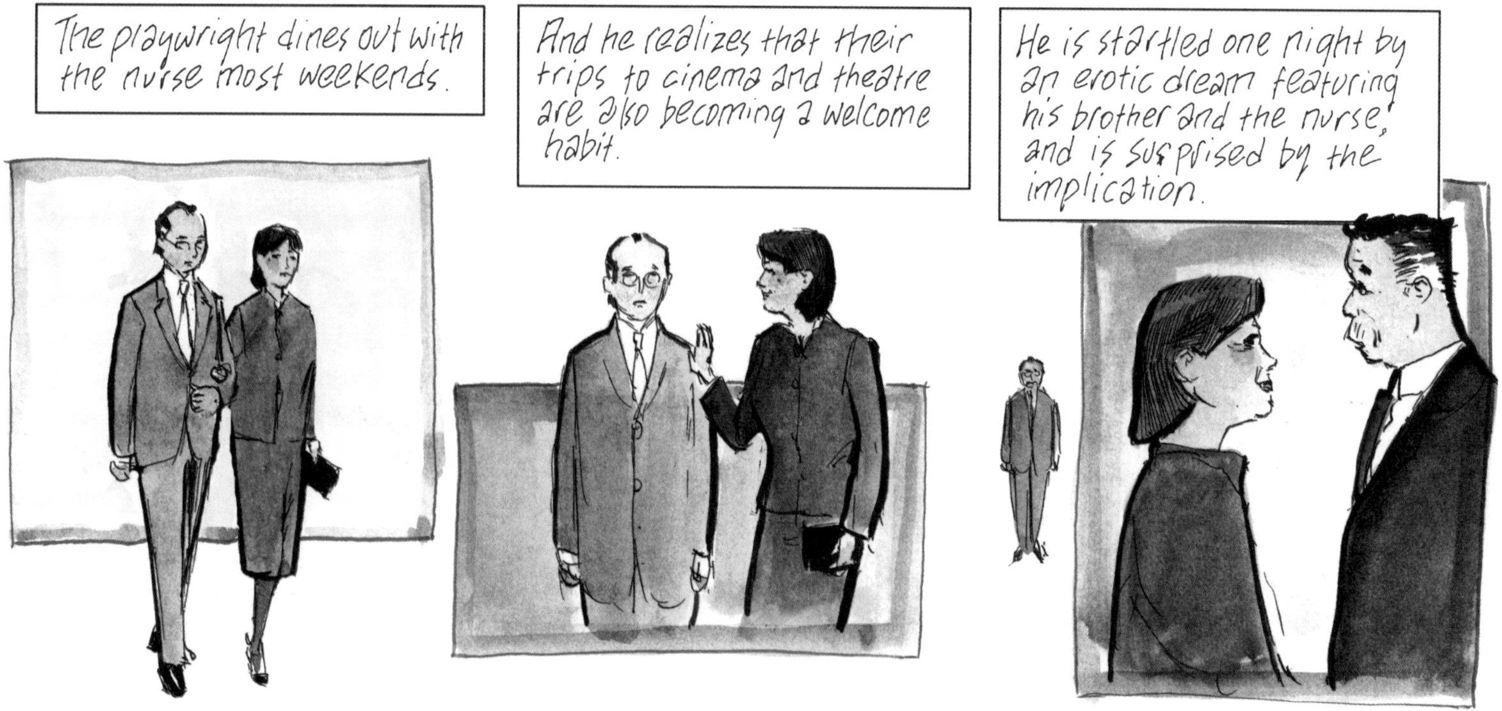
The playwright dines out with the nurse most weekends.
And he realizes that their trips to cinema and theatre are also becoming a welcome habit.
He is startled one night by an erotic dream featuring his brother and the nurse, and is surprised by the implication.

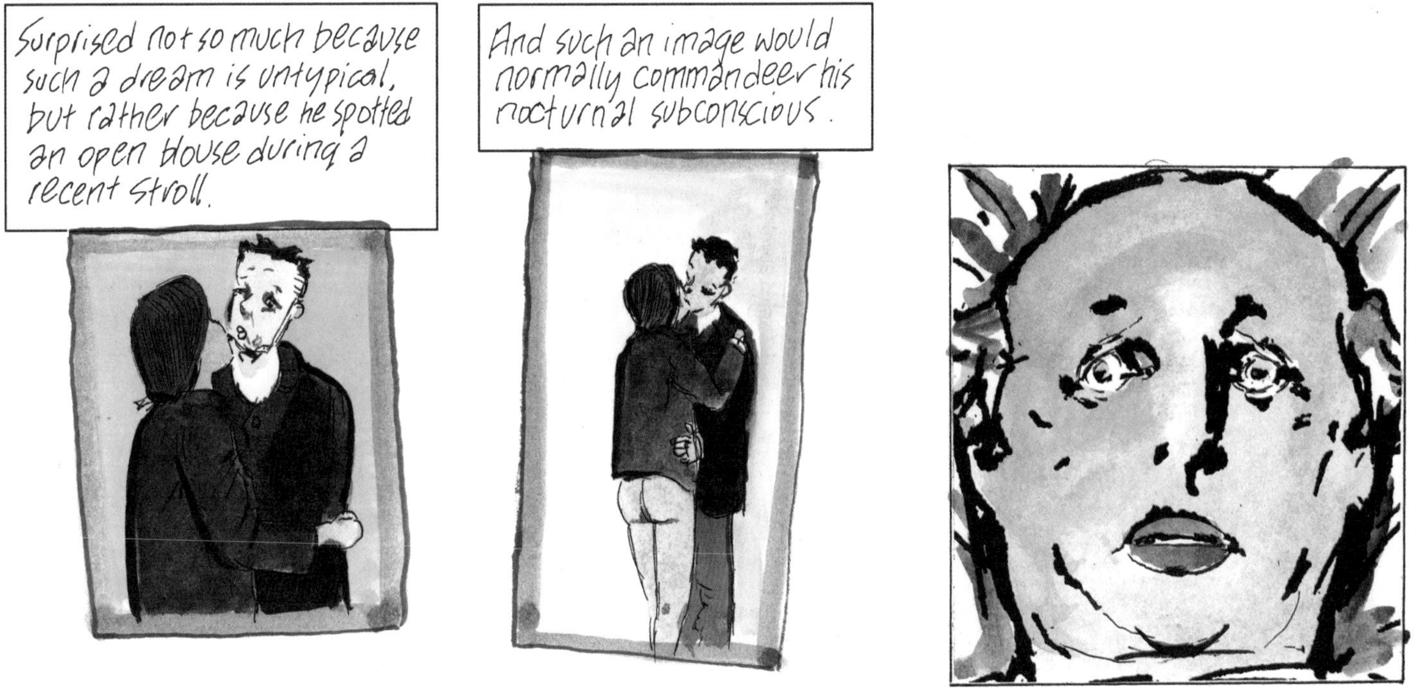
Surprised not so much because such a dream is untypical, but rather because he spotted an open blouse during a recent stroll.
And such an image would normally commandeer his nocturnal subconscious.

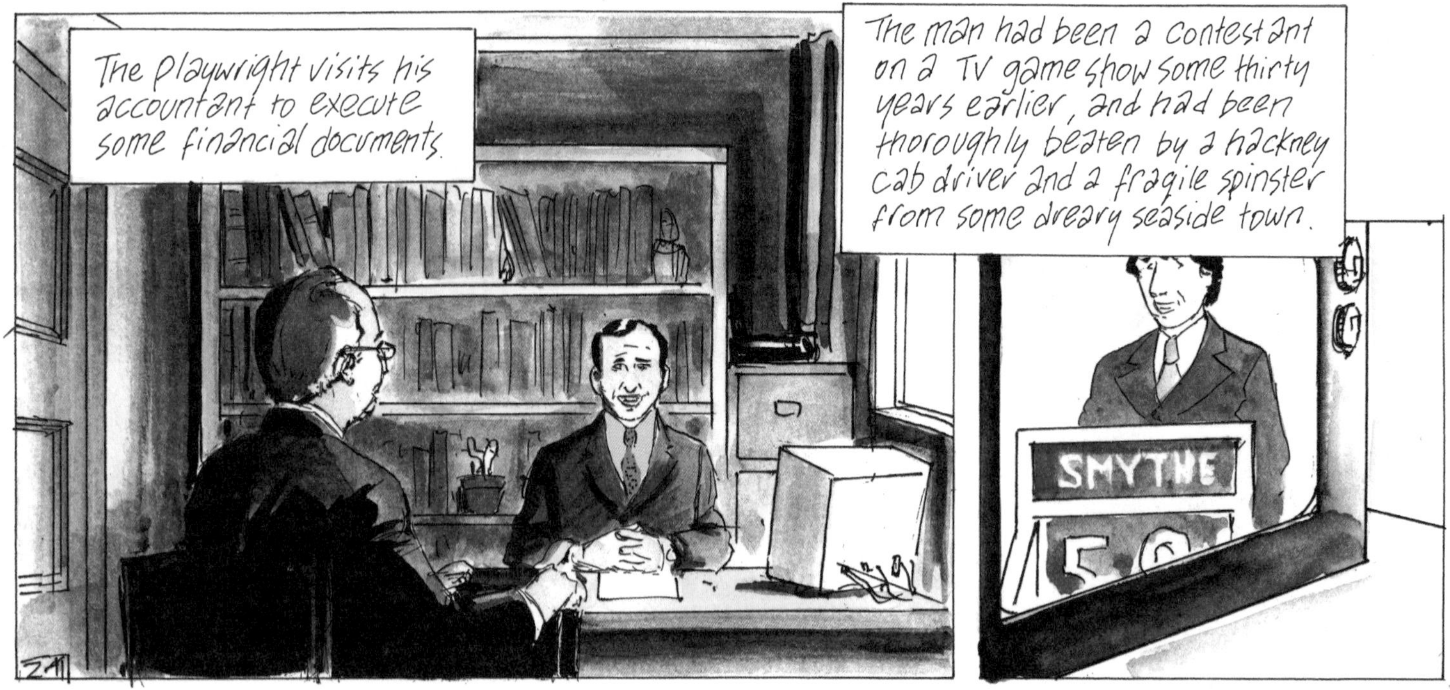
The playwright visits his accountant to execute some financial documents.
The man had been a contestant on a TV game show some thirty years earlier, and had been thoroughly beaten by a hackney cab driver and a fragile spinster from some dreary seaside town.
SMYTHE

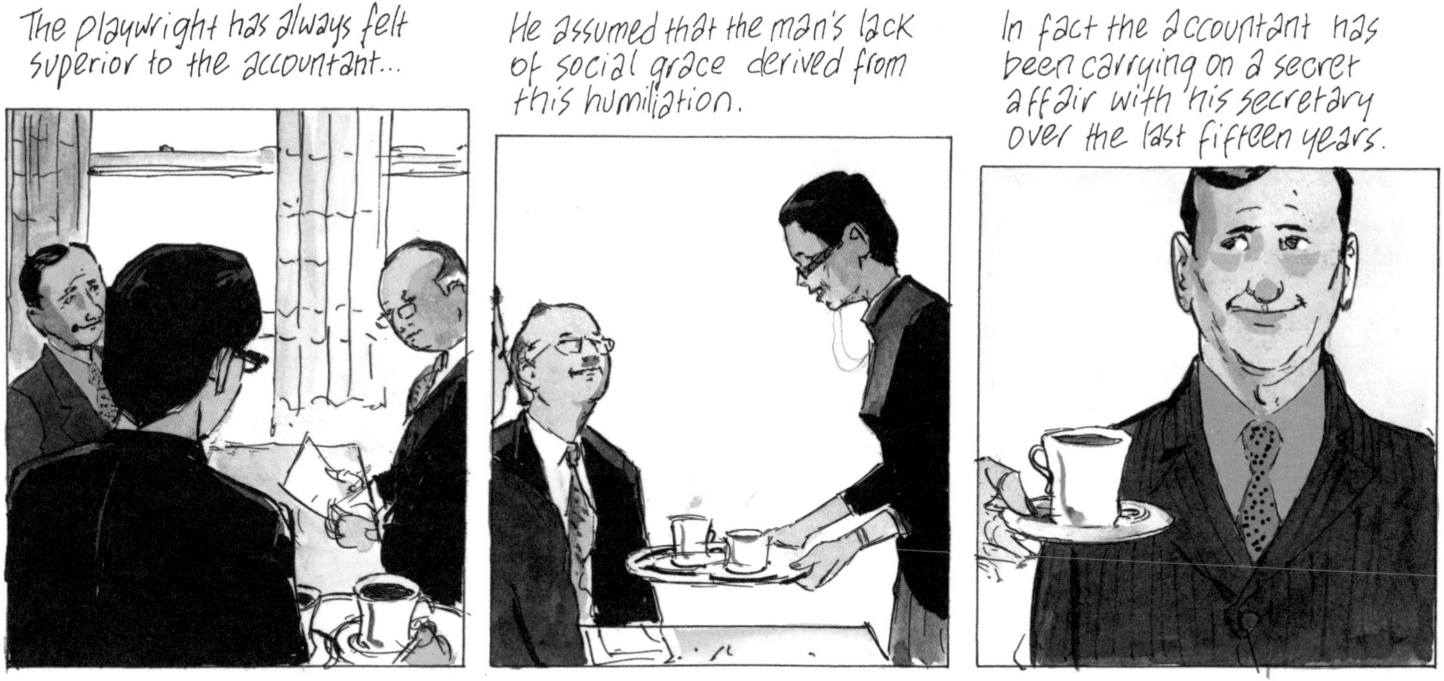
The playwright has always felt superior to the accountant...
He assumed that the man's lack of social grace derived from this humiliation.
In fact the accountant has been carrying on a secret affair with his secretary over the last fifteen years.

The irony is that the secretary isn't married, but they have conducted the relationship illicitly just to add a little extra excitement.

The playwright observes the pair glance at each other while she serves the tea and biscuits, and their secret seems blatantly obvious.

He feels like a dunce for being oblivious to the charade, but experiences a vicarious thrill at the delicious nature of their deceit.

The nurse is worried that the passing of the playwright's brother will result in the redundancy of her services.

She is surprised at how cozy their lives have become and enjoys the increasingly frequent outings.

She still refers to him as Mr. Benge, although more as a shared joke than to stand on ceremony, and he has called her Patricia for quite some time.

129

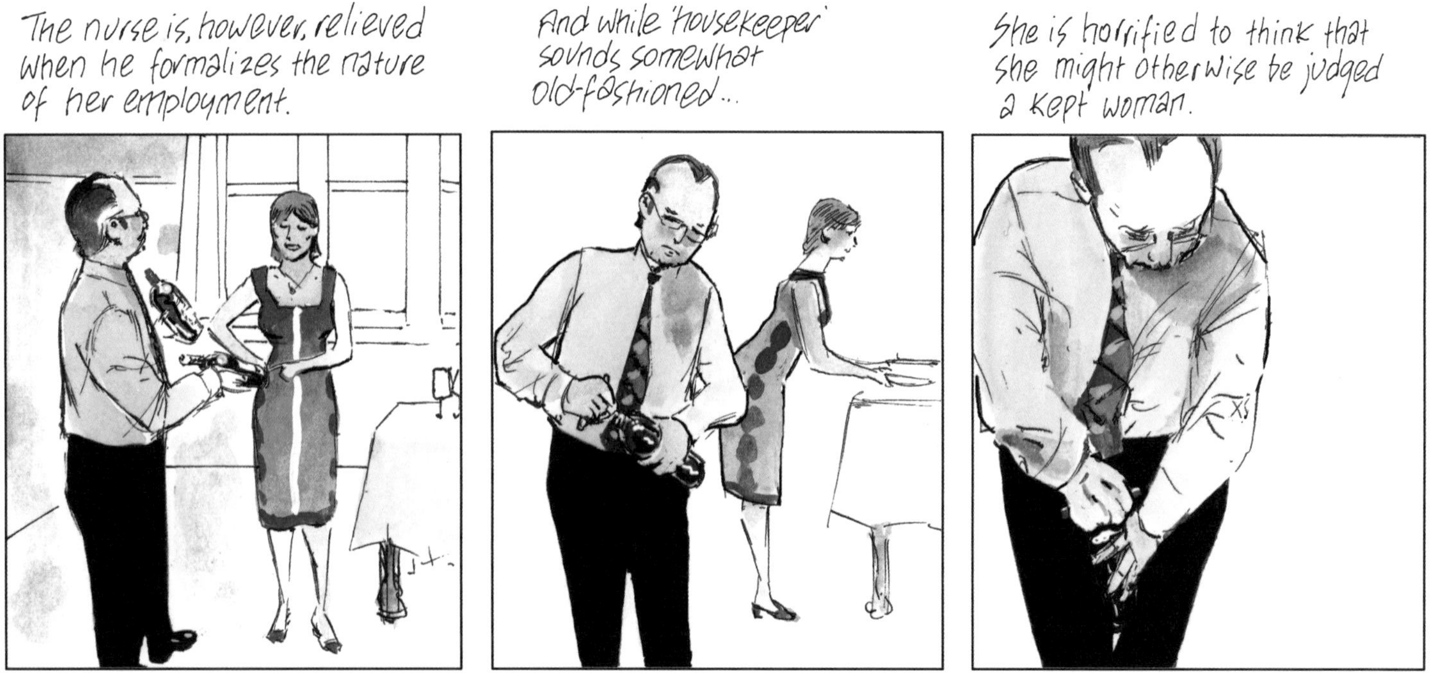
The nurse is, however, relieved when he formalizes the nature of her employment.
And while 'housekeeper' sounds somewhat old-fashioned...
She is horrified to think that she might otherwise be judged a kept woman.

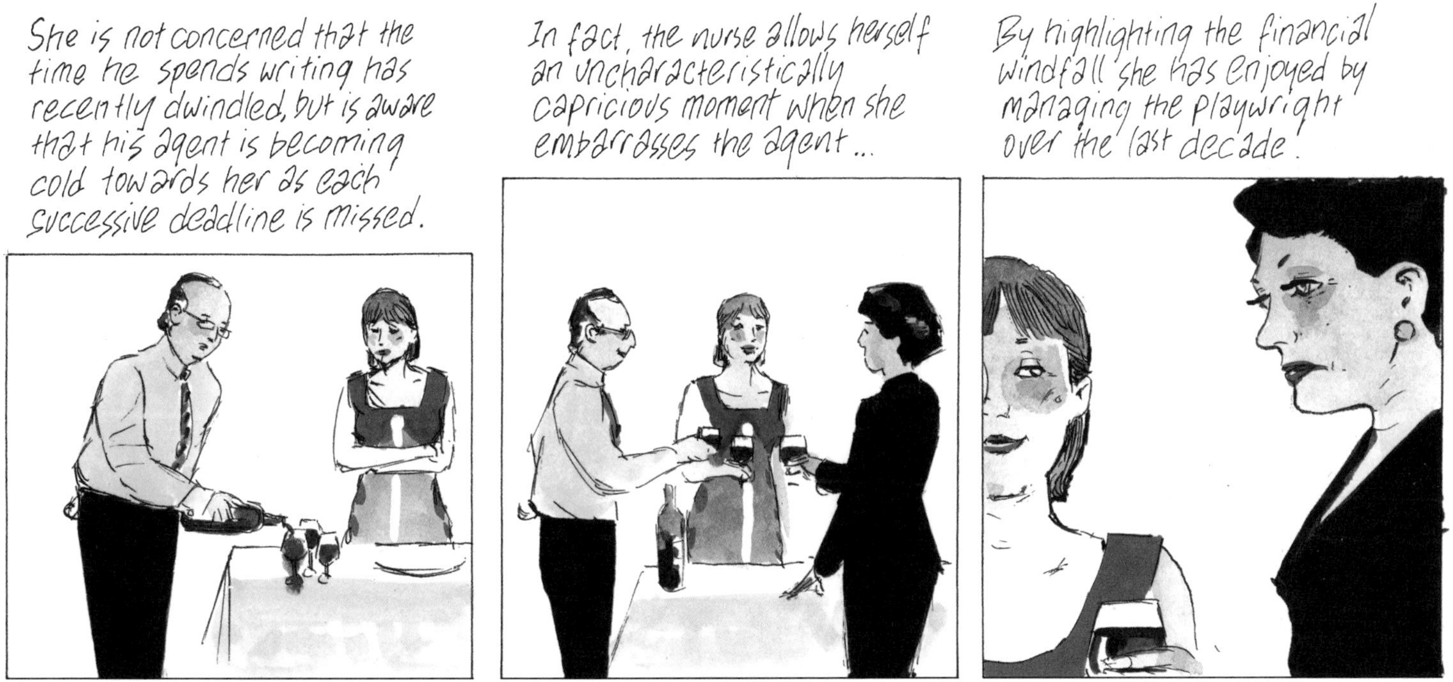
She is not concerned that the time he spends writing has recently dwindled, but is aware that his agent is becoming cold towards her as each successive deadline is missed.
In fact, the nurse allows herself an uncharacteristically capricious moment when she embarrasses the agent...
By highlighting the financial windfall she has enjoyed by managing the playwright over the last decade.

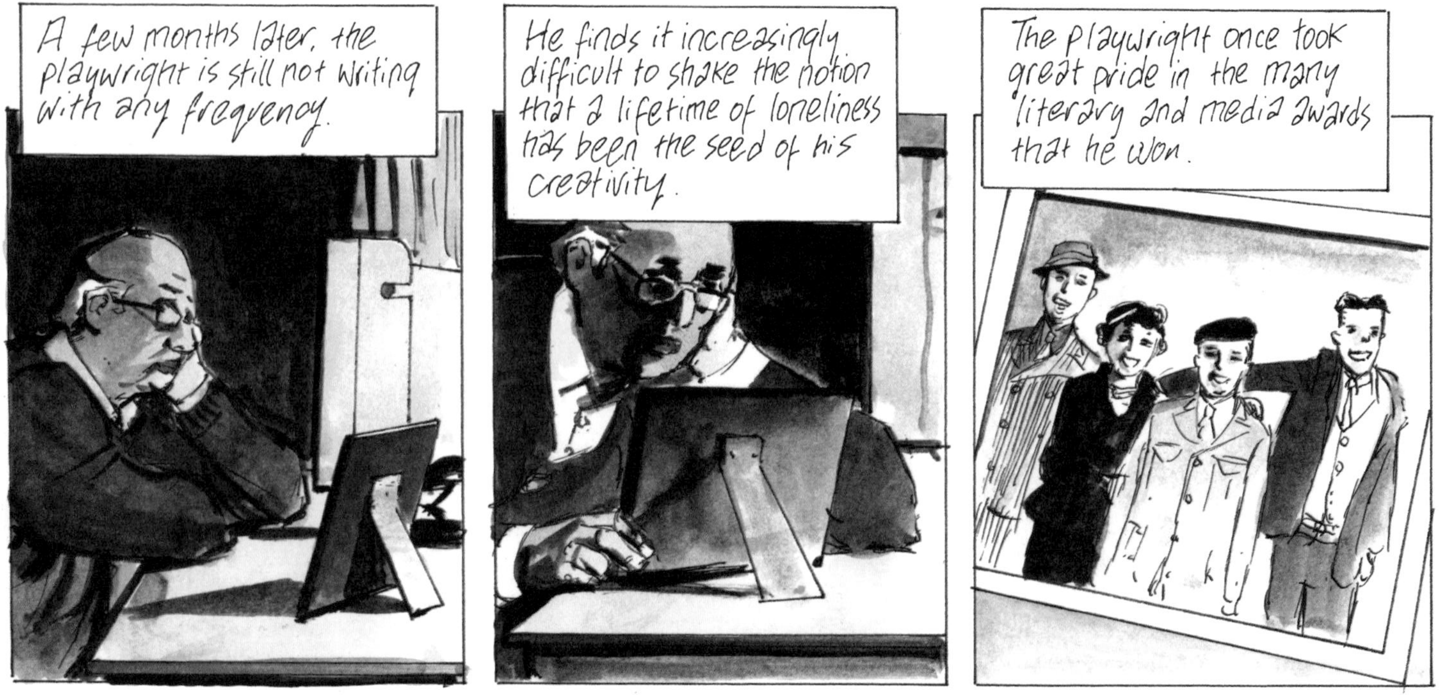
A few months later, the playwright is still not writing with any frequency.
He finds it increasingly difficult to shake the notion that a lifetime of loneliness has been the seed of his creativity.
The playwright once took great pride in the many literary and media awards that he won.

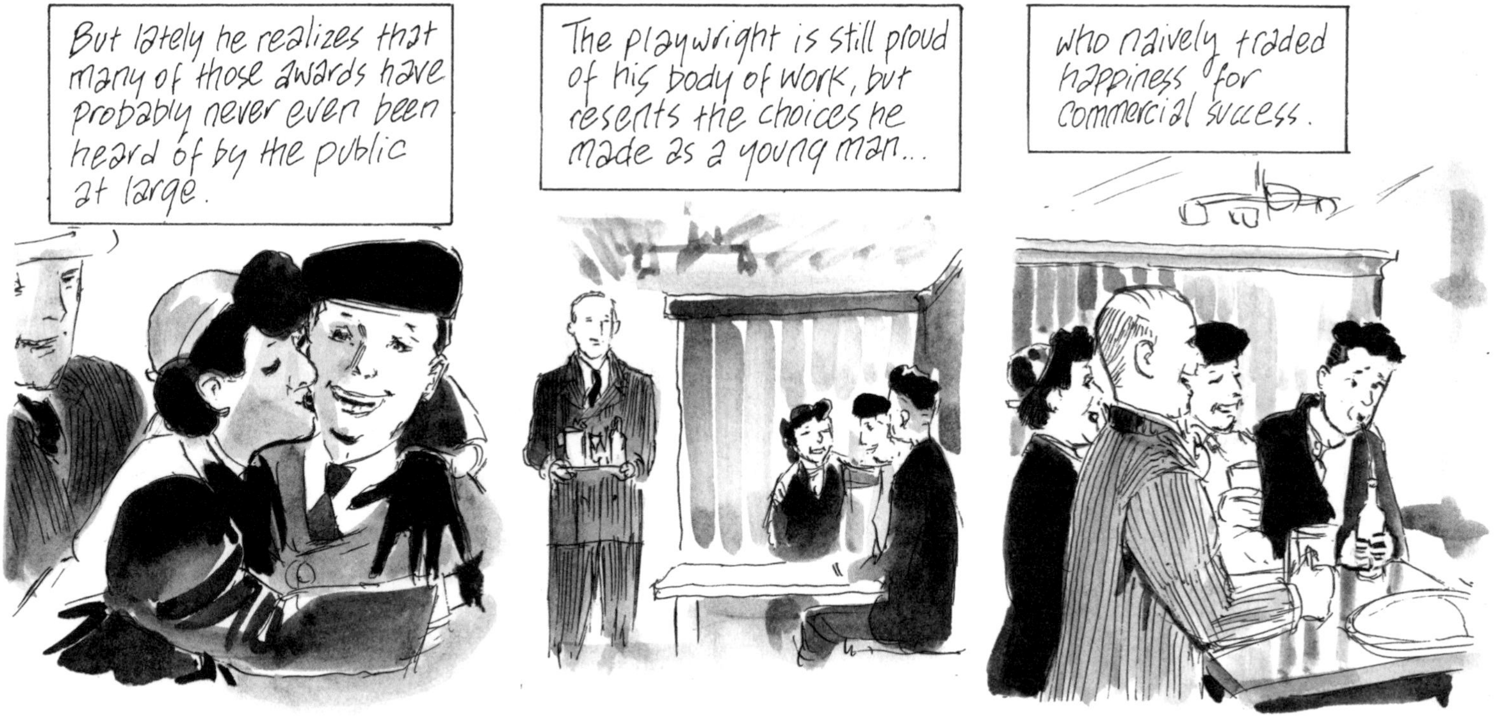
But lately he realizes that many of those awards have probably never even been heard of by the public at large.
The playwright is still proud of his body of work, but resents the choices he made as a young man...
who naively traded happiness for commercial success.

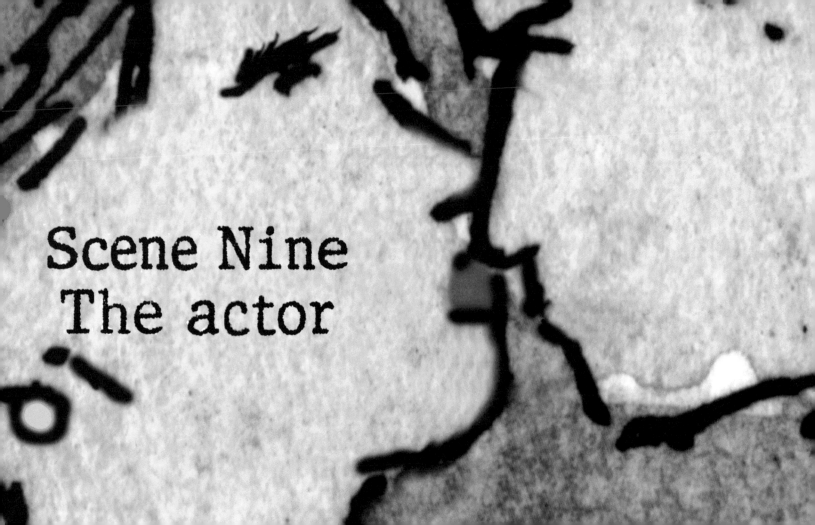

Scene Nine
The actor

The playwright's award-winning stage play, 'Tea for One', has recently been adapted to film.

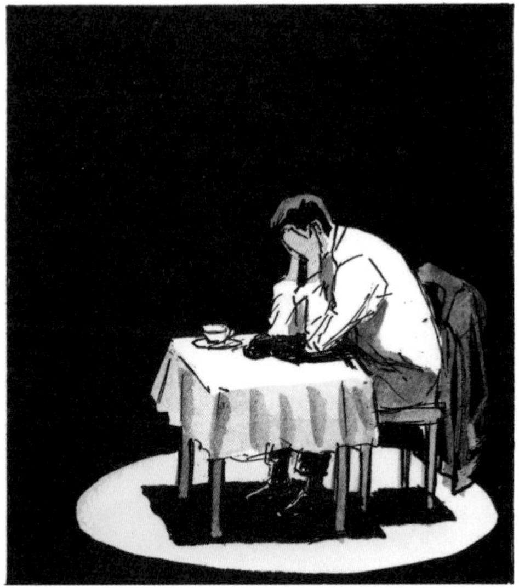

It is sufficiently successful that the lead actor has been courted by a major Hollywood producer.

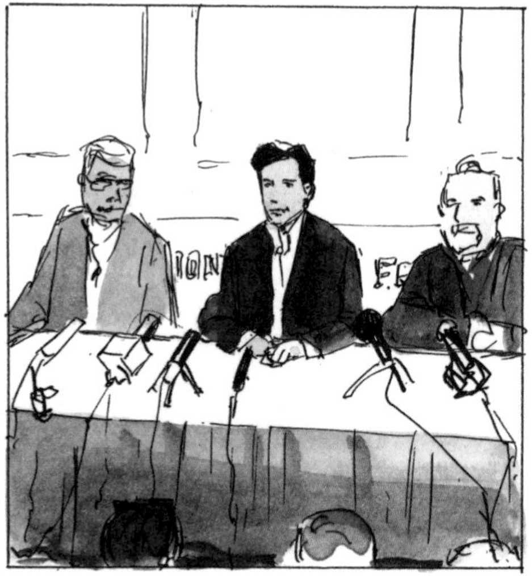

The actor arranges a thank-you dinner at an exclusive London restaurant, the chef of which is well known from an explosive fly-on-the-wall TV documentary.

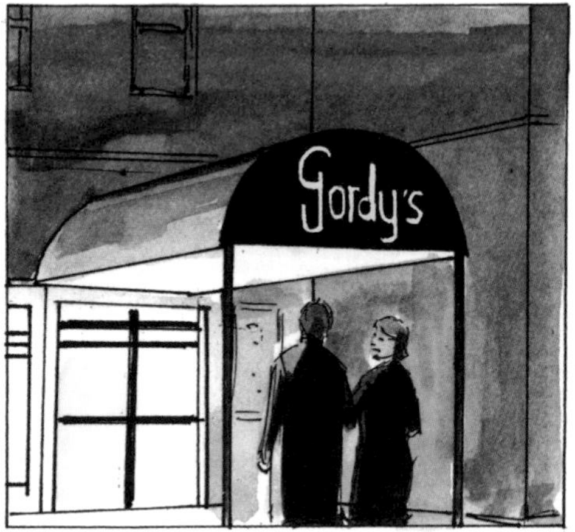
Gordy's

The actor is best known in the industry for being extremely well endowed.

Consequently he is very willing to include full-frontal nudity in much of his work.

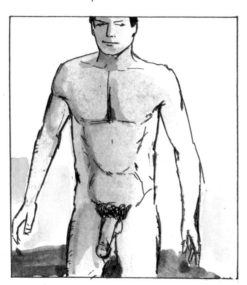

In fact, were the playwright to ghostwrite the man's autobiography, he would probably title it 'The Right Part for the Part.'

The actor is most charming in the flesh.

He mesmerizes both the playwright's agent and the nurse, with many humorous anecdotes...

Most of which centre on his famous part, playfully referred to as "Bonaparte".

The playwright notices that both women kissed him full on the lips when saying goodnight.

During the taxi ride home the nurse comments that he appeared much taller in real life than on the screen.

This observation seems odd, given that they all spent most of the evening sitting.

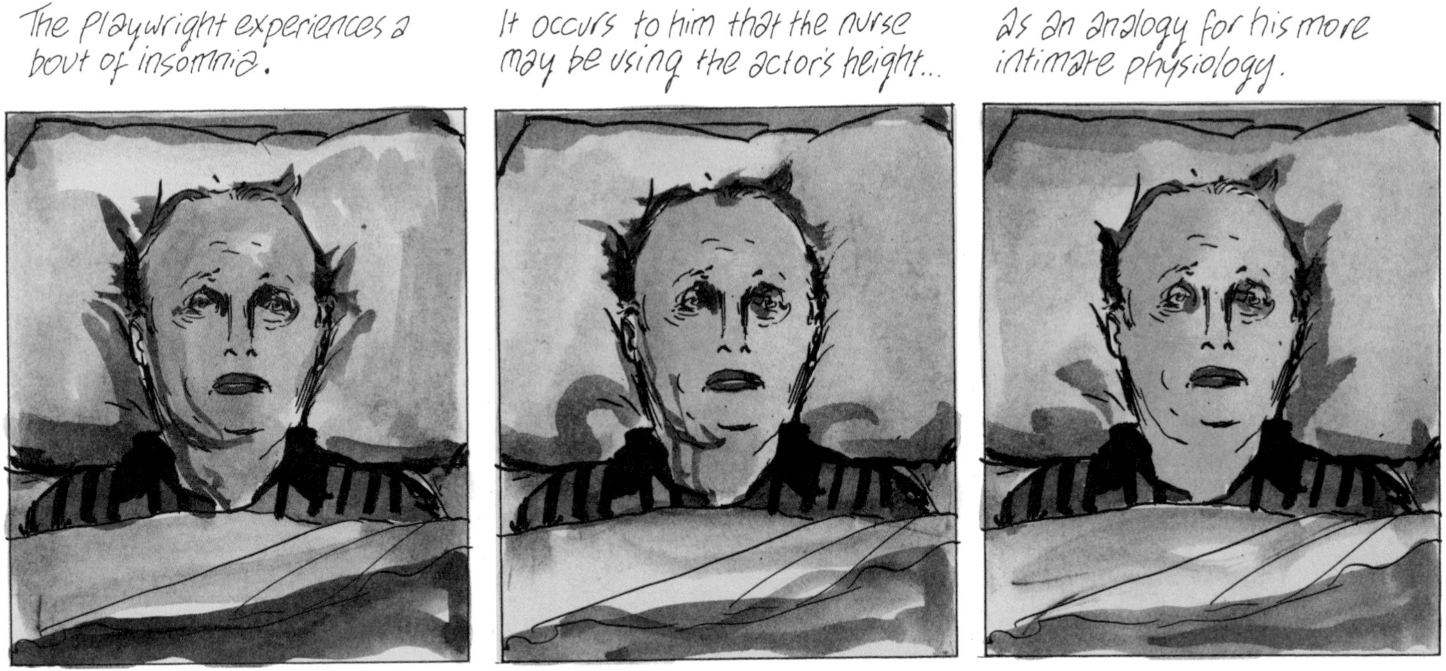
The playwright experiences a bout of insomnia.
It occurs to him that the nurse may be using the actor's height...
as an analogy for his more intimate physiology.

However, a late-night Internet search confirms that both men are in fact identical in height.

It also turns up considerable evidence suggesting that the actor is a closet homosexual.

Taking comfort from this information he drifts off to sleep.

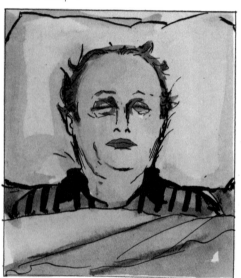

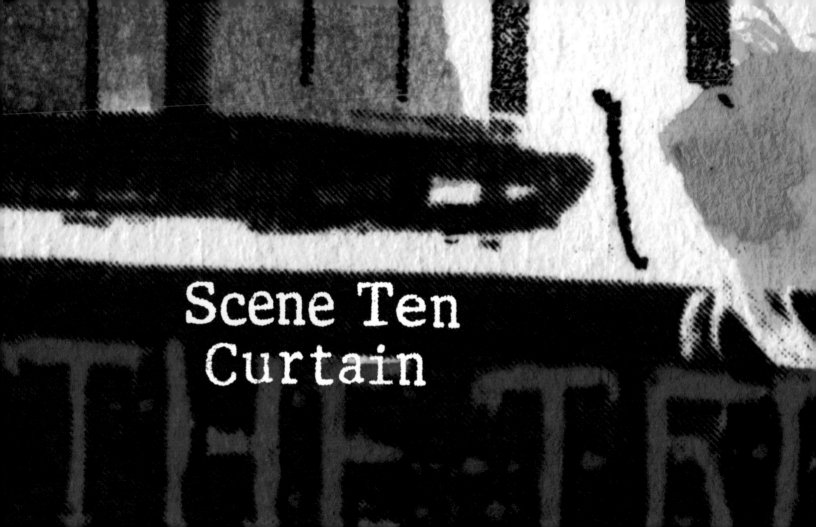

Scene Ten
Curtain

Nurse!
NO!
I said
PRICK
his
BOIL

Oddly enough, of his many creative ventures, it is the playwright's long-held interest in saucy seaside postcards that comes closest to being revived.

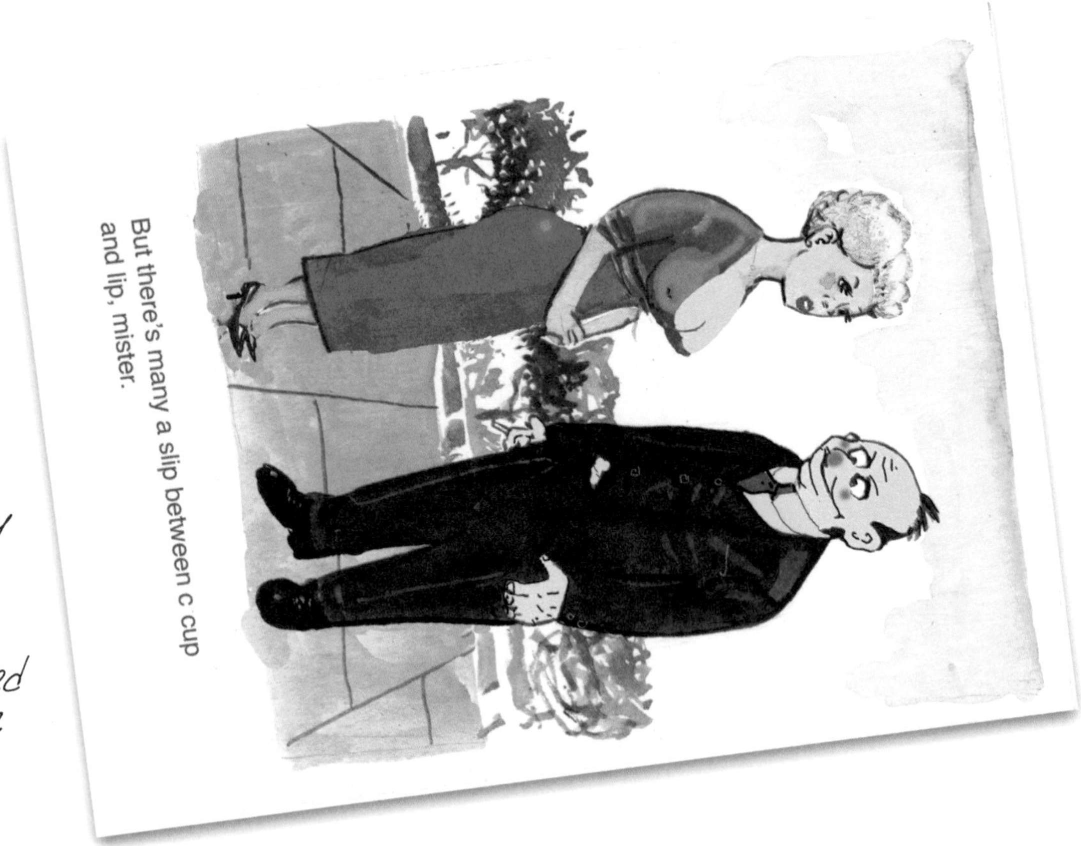
But there's many a slip between c cup
and lip, mister.

George Orwell's essay about Donald McGill piqued his interest as a youth and he has often considered writing an extensive text on the subject.

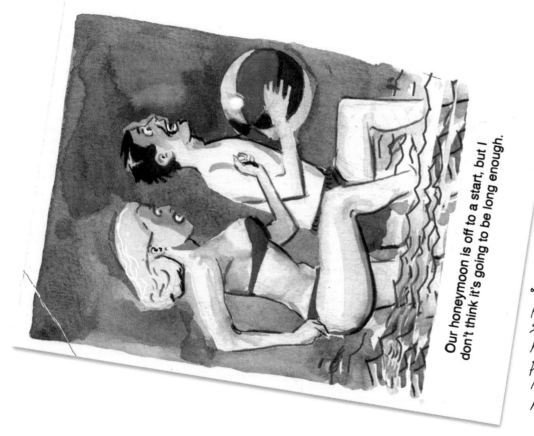

Our honeymoon is off to a start, but I don't think it's going to be long enough.

In fact, the playwright's first professional sales were single-gag ideas which he sold to a novelty publisher after returning home from his national service.

The publisher subsequently requested more explicit material for syndication to a range of gentlemen's magazines, but he declined the offer, fearing that sexual inexperience would eventually trip him up.

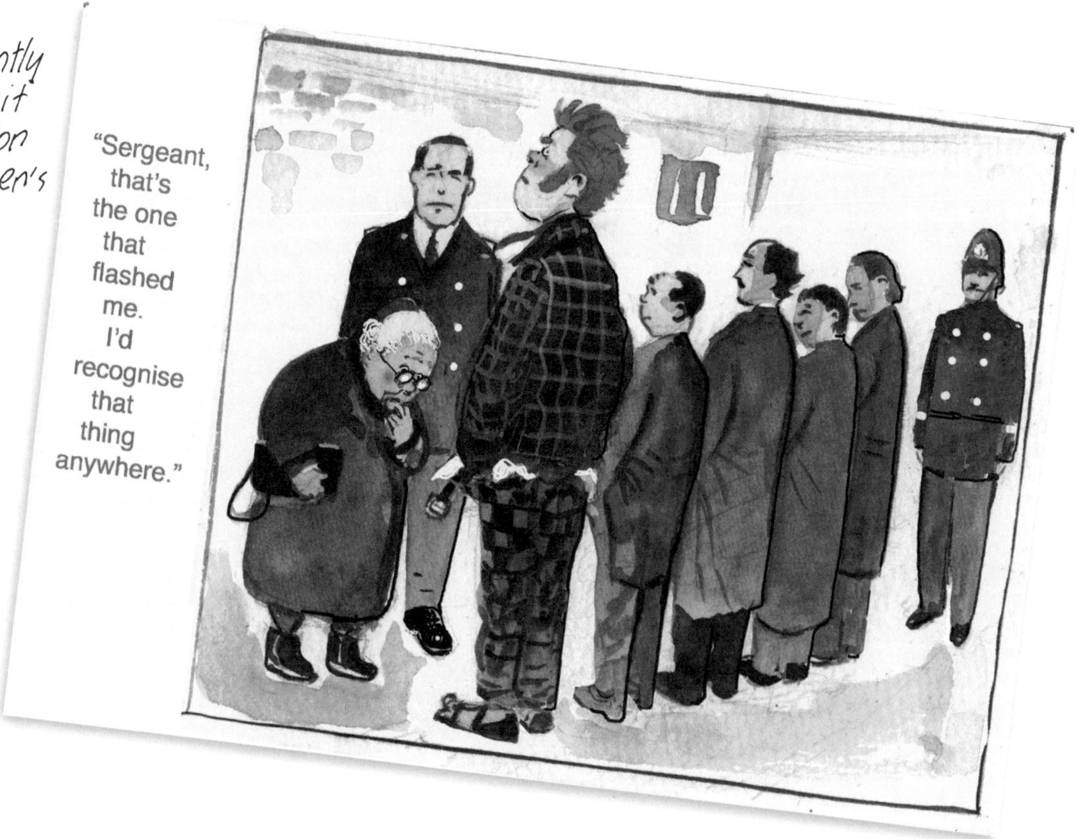
"Sergeant, that's the one that flashed me. I'd recognise that thing anywhere."

The Playwright stares at the blank page for almost an hour before concluding that he has nothing to say.

His most original idea in months was to attempt to write his new story on the original typewriter he had used at the start of his career.

He retrieved the typewriter from the attic and spent three weeks locating an enthusiast experienced in servicing his 1950's model.

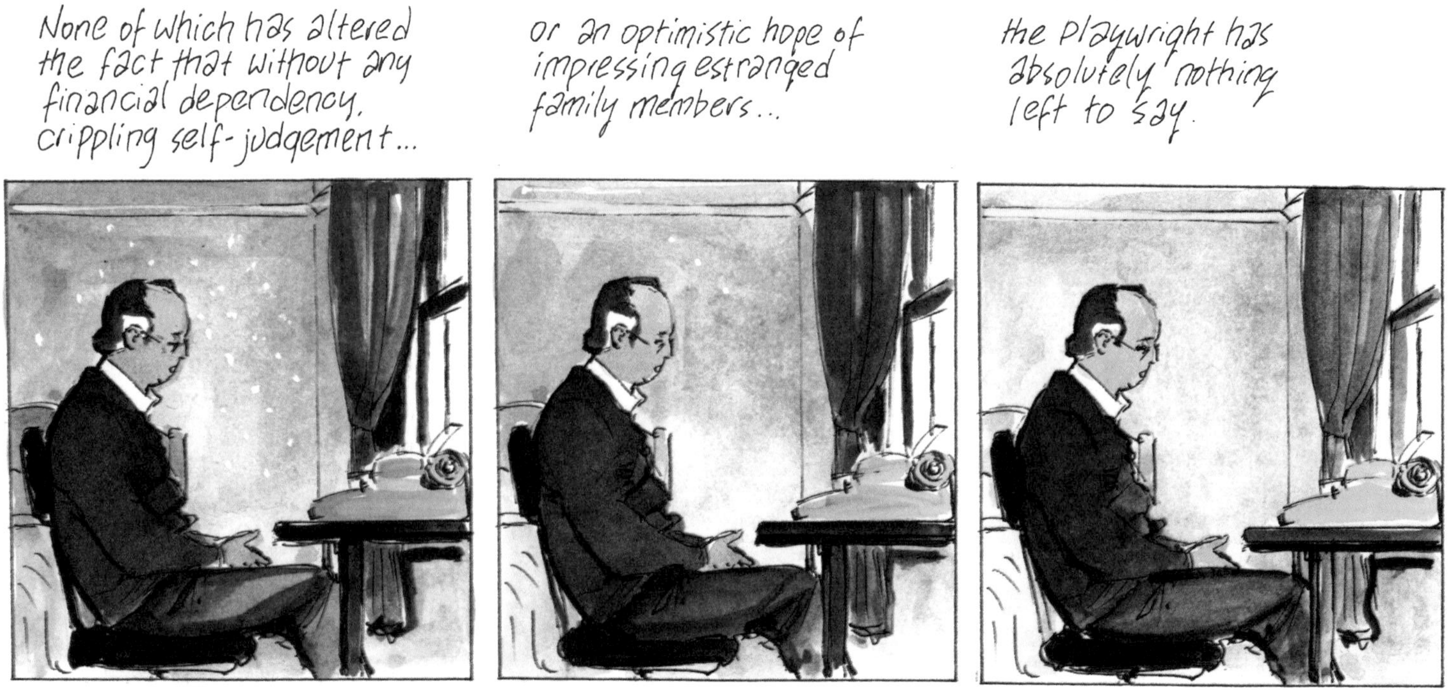
None of which has altered the fact that without any financial dependency, crippling self-judgement...
or an optimistic hope of impressing estranged family members...
the playwright has absolutely nothing left to say.

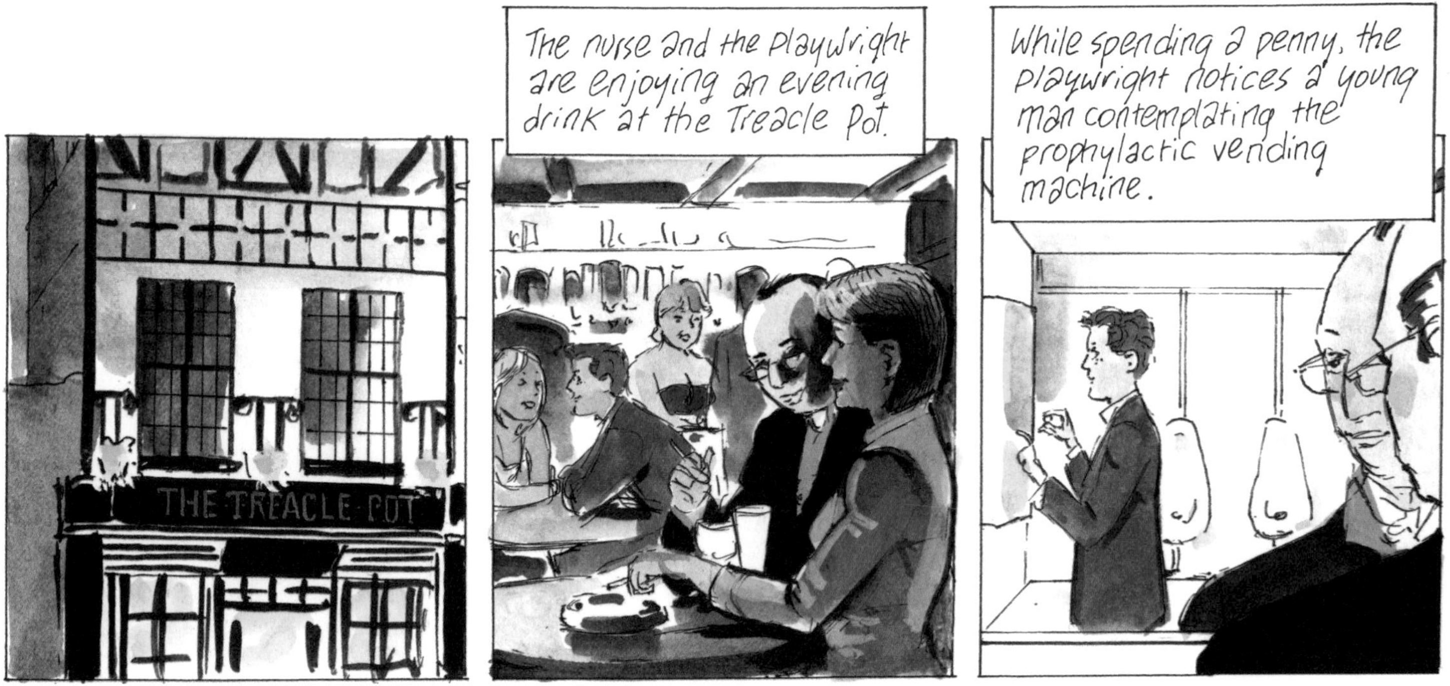
THE TREACLE POT
The nurse and the playwright are enjoying an evening drink at the Treacle Pot.
While spending a penny, the playwright notices a young man contemplating the prophylactic vending machine.

The teenage lad is clearly embarrassed. The playwright gives him an encouraging nod, largely because he also faces the same daunting challenge.

The playwright feels a connection with his newly established Kinsman and finds himself ordering the same bottle of imported lager as his young peer.

This should have tipped off the nurse that something is afoot, because he is strictly a wine drinker.

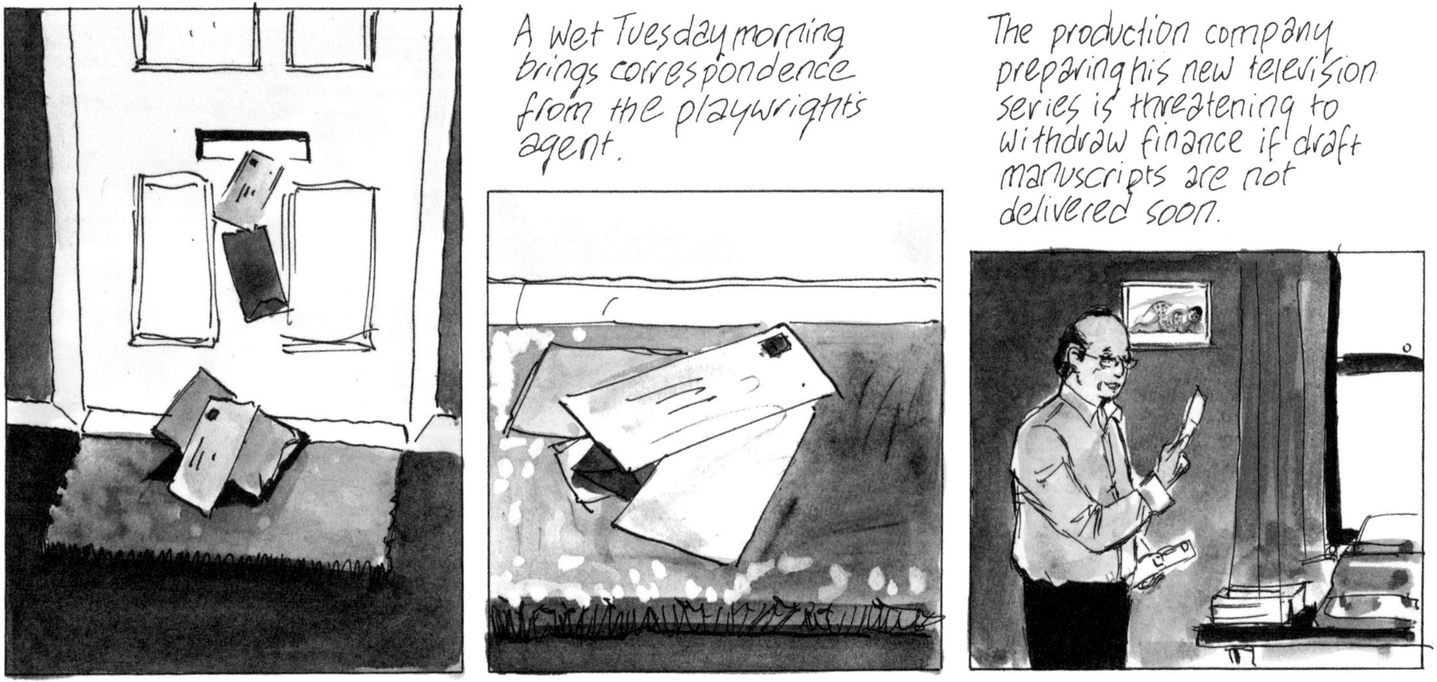
A wet Tuesday morning brings correspondence from the playwright's agent.
The production company preparing his new television series is threatening to withdraw finance if draft manuscripts are not delivered soon.

The playwright assembled the proposal in an hour at home alone, during the nurse's recent visit to a gallery opening.

The nurse returned with a gift of a small original McGill sketch...

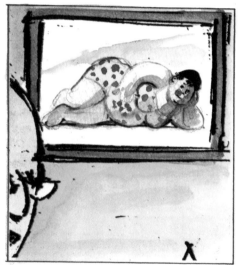

Stunning the playwright with the gift's perfection, intimacy, and, no doubt, fiscal value.

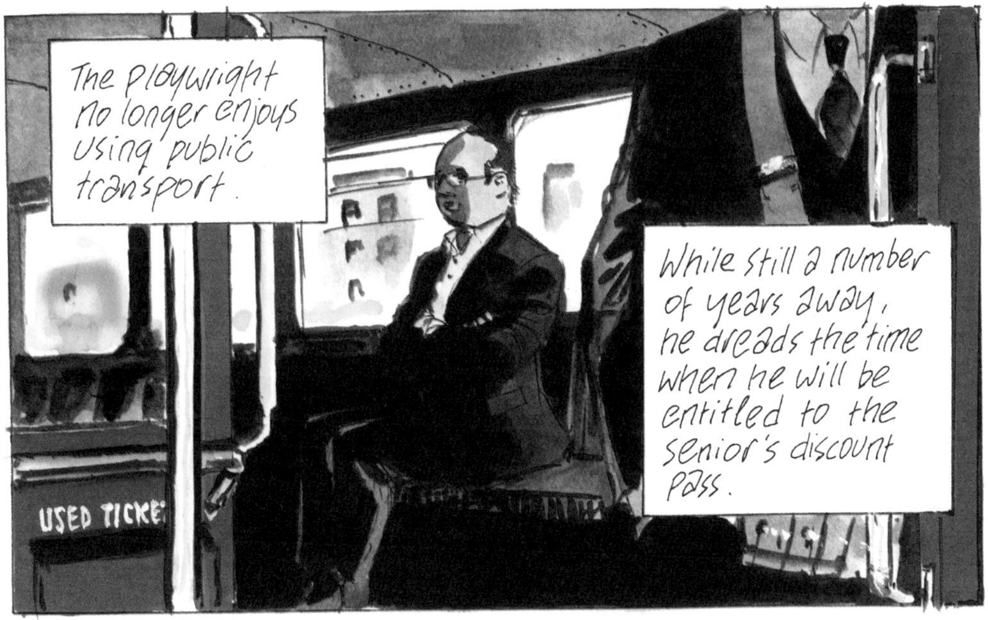
The playwright no longer enjoys using public transport.
While still a number of years away, he dreads the time when he will be entitled to the senior's discount pass.
USED TICKE

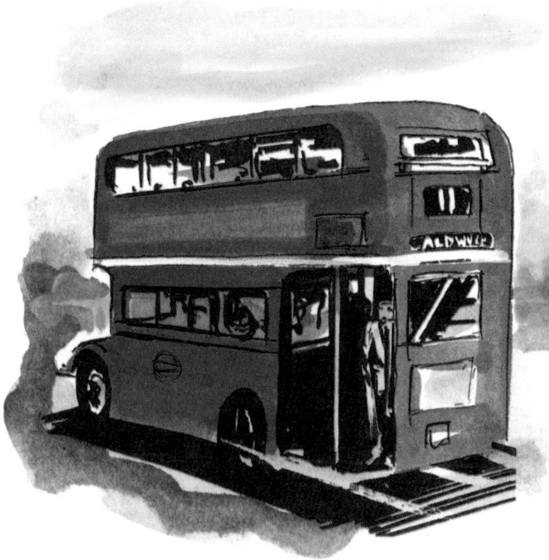

The playwright has a notion that a driving holiday through the Champagne region will make a nice Easter break.

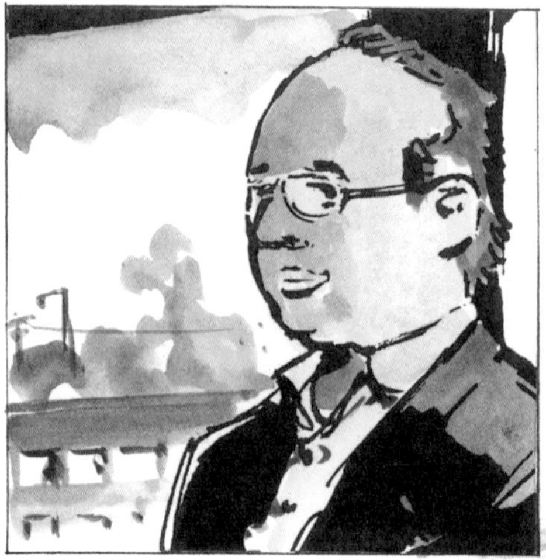

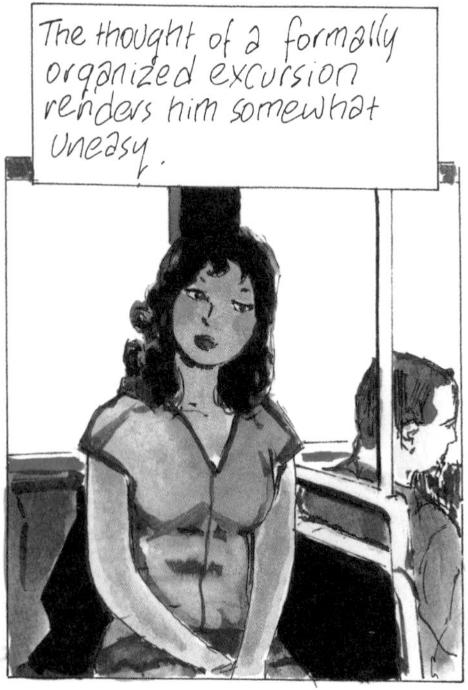
The thought of a formally organized excursion renders him somewhat uneasy.

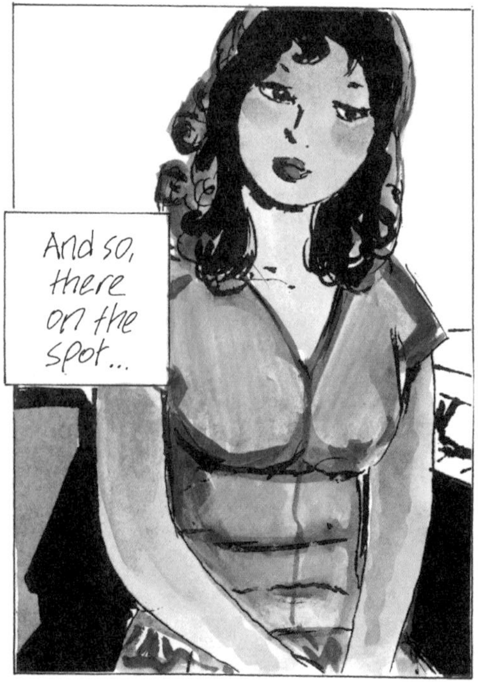
And so, there on the spot...

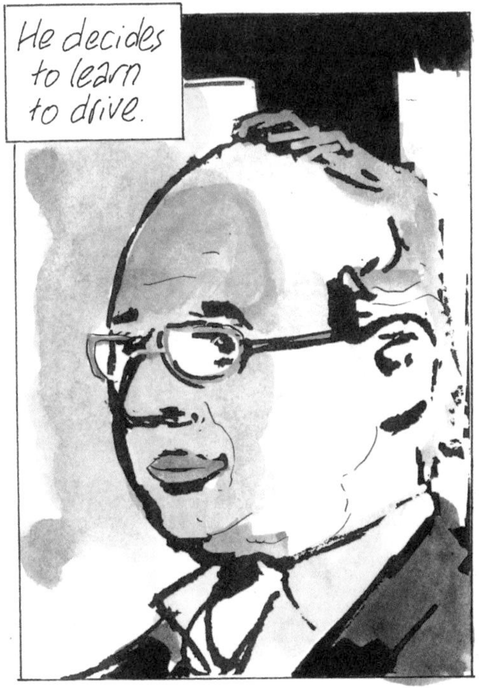
He decides to learn to drive.

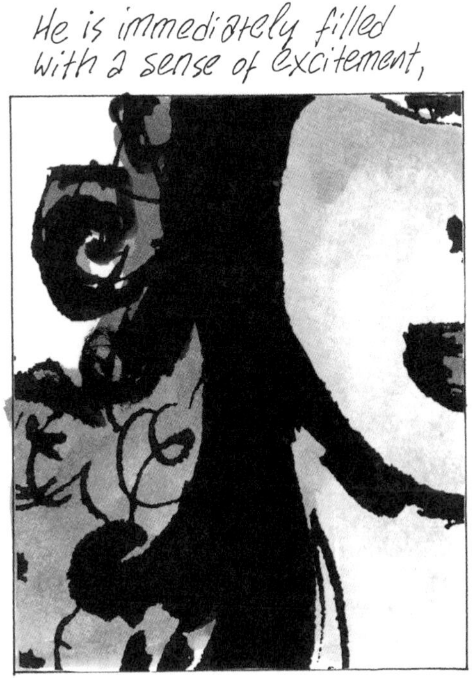
He is immediately filled with a sense of excitement,

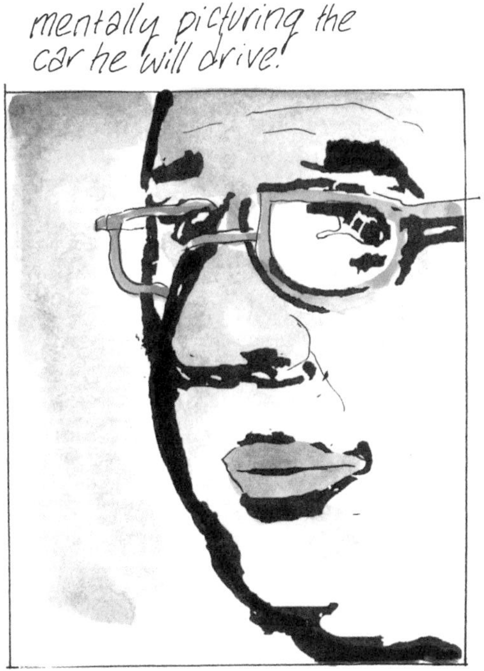
mentally picturing the car he will drive.

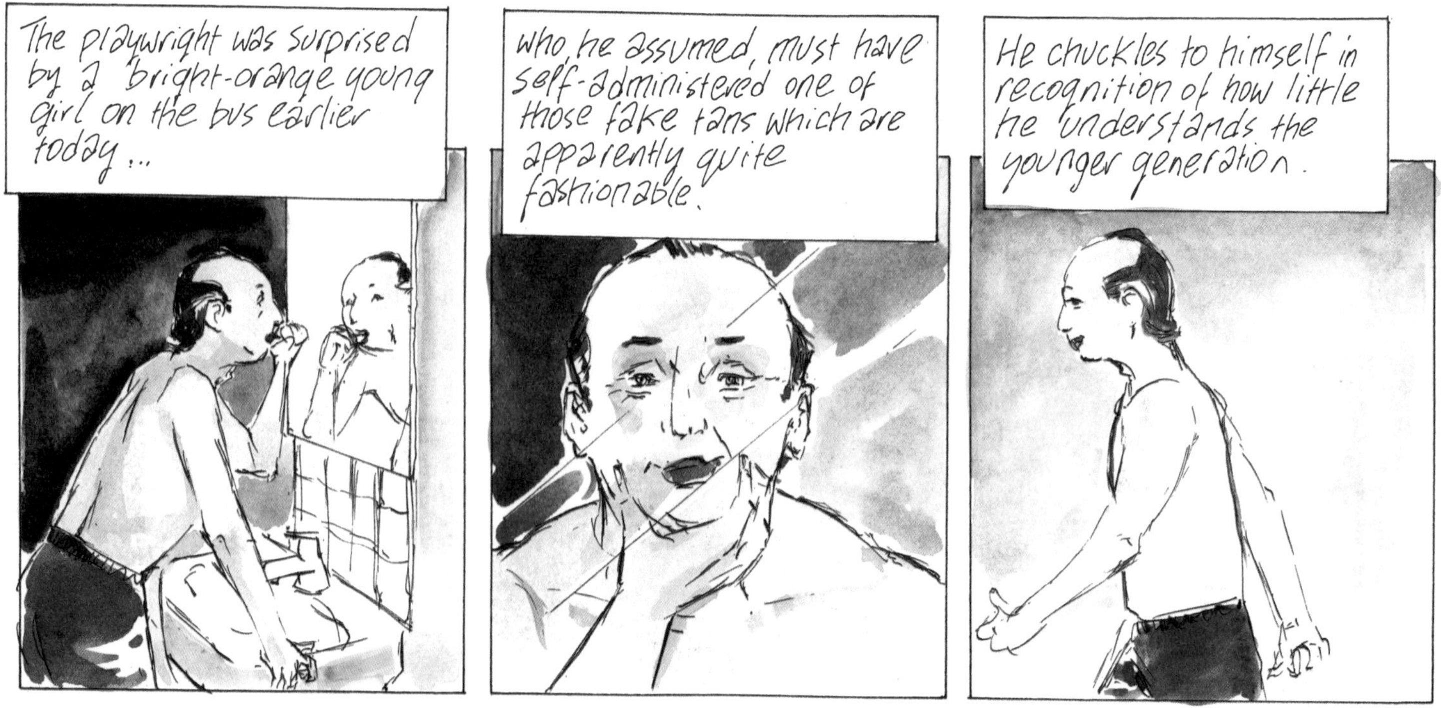
The playwright was surprised by a bright-orange young girl on the bus earlier today...
who, he assumed, must have self-administered one of those fake tans which are apparently quite fashionable.
He chuckles to himself in recognition of how little he understands the younger generation.

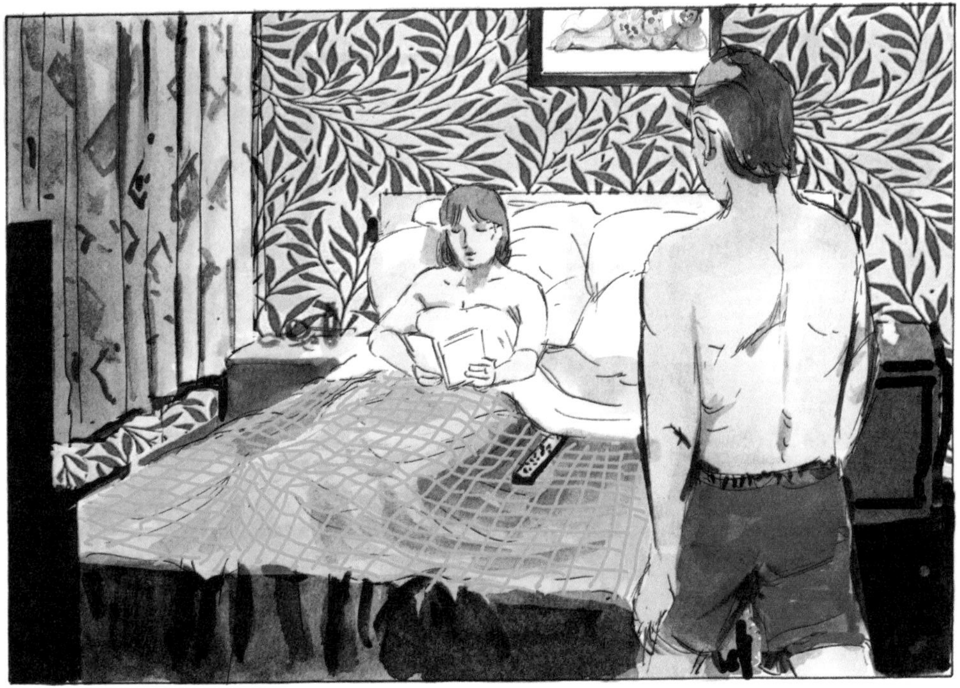

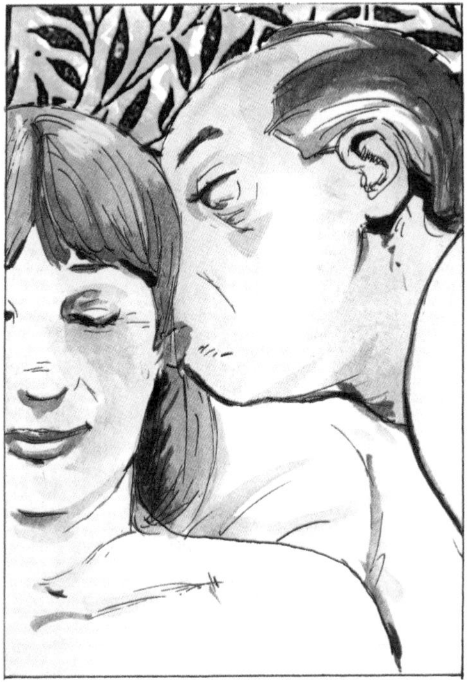

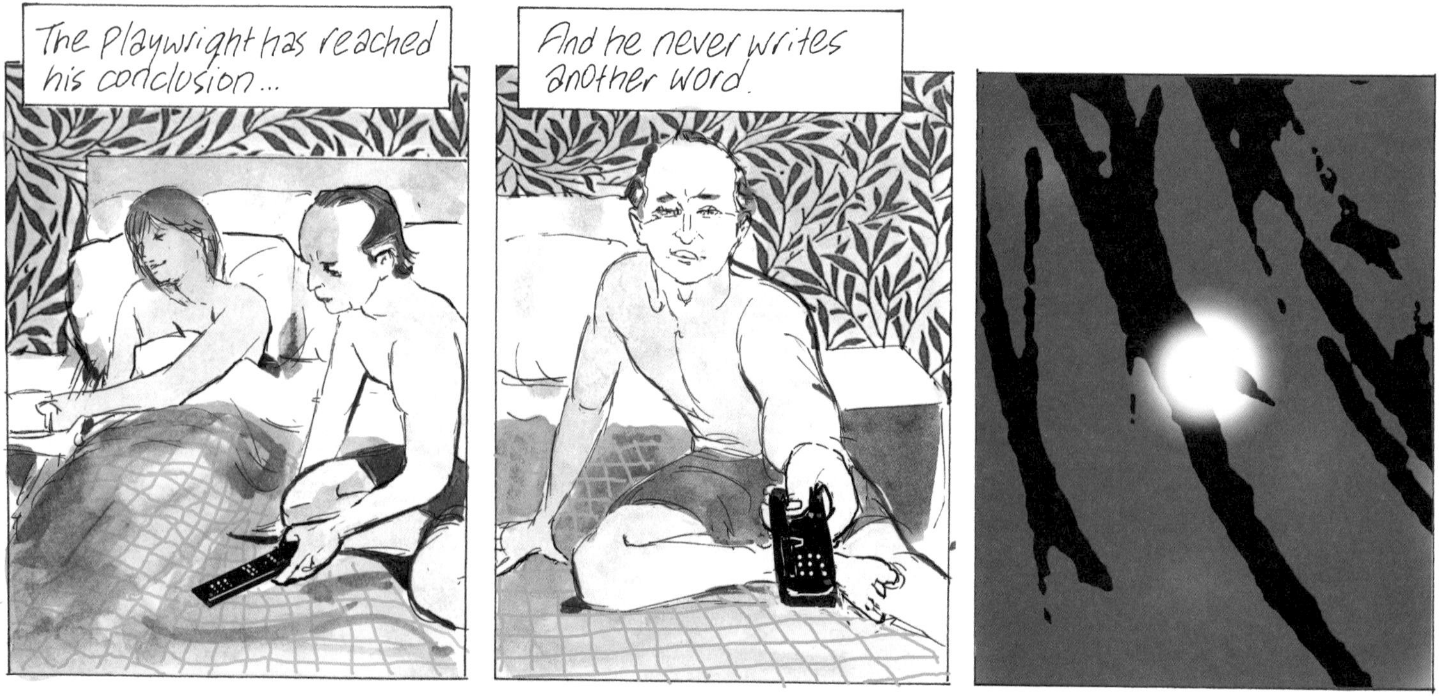
The playwright has reached his conclusion...
And he never writes another word.

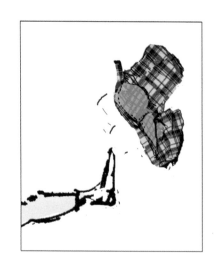

Eddie Campbell and Daren White are expatriate Britons living in Brisbane, Australia. They first met in 1993.

Campbell's credits include the hefty tomes FROM HELL (with Alan Moore), ALEC: THE YEARS HAVE PANTS and A DISEASE OF LANGUAGE (with Alan Moore), as well as the full-color books THE FATE OF THE ARTIST, THE BLACK DIAMOND DETECTIVE AGENCY and THE AMAZING REMARKABLE MONSIEUR LEOTARD.

Daren White is the editor of the Australian anthology, DEEVEE. He has written for a number of Australian publications, including Campbell's BACCHUS magazine, and for DC and Dark Horse Comics in the US. He is also a Chartered Accountant.

The two have worked together on a numbers of projects, including GOTHAM EMERGENCY and BATMAN: THE ORDER OF BEASTS, which was Campbell's first full-color book.